Howard Rayner

Dawn over the outback

AF179001

Ernst Klett Verlag
Stuttgart · Leipzig

Contents

Before you read

Multiple choice

Look at the map on the back of this reader and make a guess.

1. How far from Darwin is Alice Springs?
   a) 1500 km ☐
   b) 700 km ☐
   c) 500 km ☐

2. The distance between Darwin and Alice Springs is the same as the distance between …
   a) Hamburg and Munich. ☐
   b) Hamburg and Rome. ☐
   c) Hamburg and Bordeaux. ☐

3. How long does it take to get from Darwin to Alice Springs by plane?
   a) 2 hours 55 minutes ☐
   b) 1 hour 55 minutes ☐
   c) 55 minutes ☐

4. How long does it take to drive from Darwin to Alice Springs by car?
   a) 20 hours ☐
   b) 15 hours ☐
   c) 10 hours ☐

5. How long would it take to walk from Darwin to Alice Springs?
   a) 14 days ☐
   b) 7 days ☐
   c) 4 days ☐

Chapter 1   The other side of the world

"Wow, each time I think I've seen all the movies I find another channel!" Pim said happily. He held up the remote control which was connected to his seat. "There are hundreds of games. This plane must have a giant
5 computer system. A couple of terabytes at least."

"I've no idea what you're talking about," Maritska said as she looked for a mirror in her shoulder bag.

"Bytes are the units of information on a computer," explained Pim. "A kilobyte is one thousand bytes –"

10 "Whatever." Maritska stopped him before he could say more. "The games are for little kids like you and all the movies are boring. The only thing I want to do is sleep."

Pim leaned back in his seat. It really annoyed him that his sister wasn't interested in the plane's technology. "You
15 can go to sleep if you want. The seat tilts all the way back like this." Pim pushed a button in the armrest. His seat dropped backwards with a sudden bump.

There was a shout from the row behind as the movement knocked the passenger's drink off his table.

20 Pim jumped up and leaned over the back of his seat. The man in the row behind was mopping spilt coffee off his trousers.

"Sorry," said Pim brightly, "I keep forgetting that when I move my seat it shakes your table."

25 "I know," replied the grumpy passenger. He had an Australian accent.

"This flight feels like it has taken a lifetime." Maritska stared at her reflection and rubbed her tired eyes. "I want to go to sleep in a bed. A real bed. My old bed."

30 "That's impossible," Pim raised his seat back. "Your old bed is fourteen thousand kilometres behind us now."

---

3 **remote contol** [rɪˈməʊt kənˌtrəʊl] Fernbedienung • 13 **to lean** [liːn] sich lehnen
• 15 **to tilt** [tɪlt] sich neigen • 19 **to knock sth off** [nɒk] etw. herunterstoßen •
21 **to spill sth** [spɪl] etw. verschütten • 23 **bright** [braɪt] fröhlich

Maritska sadly stared at the map on the video screen. It showed a small, white plane with a long, red trail. The trail showed how far they had flown. It crossed Indonesia and India and went all the way back to Dubai, the place this flight had left twelve hours ago. The flight they were on before was from Amsterdam to Dubai. That journey had taken seven hours.

"It's so exciting! We've travelled half way around the world!" Pim jumped up and down in his seat. The movement rattled the breakfast tray of the man in the seat behind. "I'm going to see a new country!"

"Hey kid, stop it!" The passenger in the seat behind got up and looked over Pim's seat. "You've not stopped wriggling and talking since we took off. How about giving me some peace and quiet?"

"Yeah, calm down," Jake put a hand on Pim's knee. "Sorry," Jake turned to the man behind, "he'll keep still for the rest of the flight."

"I wasn't doing anything." Pim folded his arms grumpily.

"It won't happen again. Will it?" Jake fixed his dark brown eyes on Pim.

"Stop bullying him," Maritska told Jake.

"You're always moaning at me," complained Pim. "I'm only a little kid. Who are you to tell me what to do?"

"Your older brother," replied Jake.

Pim and Maritska looked at each other and both gave a small laugh.

"I'm so bored, I give in. Show me how this stupid game thing works." Maritska pulled a remote control out of her armrest and passed it to Pim.

Pim's bad mood disappeared at once as he began to teach his sister how to handle the plane's entertainment system.

---

10 **to rattle** [ˌrætl] klappern • 10 **tray** [treɪ] Tablett • 14 **to wriggle** [ˈrɪgl] sich winden • 19 **to fold** [fəʊld] verschränken • 20 **to fix** [fɪks] *hier:* richten • 23 **to moan** [məʊn] klagen, sich beschweren

Jake plumped up his pillow and leant his head against the plane window. Pim and Maritska's talking slowly disappeared into the background as he stared down at the endless ocean. Through the clouds he saw tiny waves
5 on the Timor Sea. It was thousands of metres below their double-deck jet.

Jake hated being the eldest in the family. A couple of years ago, just after his fourteenth birthday, their parents had begun working far away from Holland. Pim, Maritska
10 and Jake went to live with their aunt and uncle who worked long hours and were not at home very often. The job of keeping Pim under control always seemed to fall on Jake. It was bad enough when Pim was ten, but since he had turned twelve Pim was always doing crazy things. Jake
15 often had to tell him off. Even if Maritska, who was fifteen, was annoyed by Pim's behaviour, she'd take her younger brother's side. They'd giggle and whisper to each other, just like they were doing now.

A great loneliness flooded over Jake. Right now, even
20 though he was among hundreds of other people on the plane, he felt like the only person on earth. Looking down at the sea, Jake wondered what his future held.

Jake was so lost in his thought he almost missed what was happening in the world outside. Suddenly he saw
25 something. "There's something below us!"

The plane vibrated violently. The overhead lockers rattled. There was a loud 'Bing!' as the 'fasten seat belts' sign lit up. The cabin crew stopped serving breakfast.

"Is it a UFO? Are we being chased by fighter planes?"
30 Pim tried to look out of the window. Maritska held on to her armrest so tightly her knuckles went white. She began to cough. After she had been sick a few years ago, she always did this whenever she was nervous.

---

1 **to plump sth up** [plʌmp] etw. aufschütteln • 1 **pillow** [ˈpɪləʊ] Kissen • 17 **to giggle** [ˈgɪɡl] kichern • 17 **to whisper** [ˈwɪspə] flüstern • 19 **to flood** [flʌd] (über) fluten • 27 **'fasten seat belts' sign** [ˌfɑːsn ˈsiːt belts saɪn] Anschnallzeichen • 31 **knuckle** [ˈnʌkl] Fingerknöchel • 32 **to cough** [kɒf] husten

"Nice guesses, but none of those," Jake said to Pim. "Don't panic, it's just a bit of turbulence," he told Maritska. He pointed to the horizon, "You should see this."

Maritska and Pim leaned over and looked out of the window. "What are we meant to be looking at?" asked 5 Pim.

"There's land in sight," replied Jake. "It's Australia."

• • •

"Ladies and gentlemen, we have arrived in Darwin. Local time is five minutes past eight in the morning," said the flight attendant over the intercom. 10

The plane engine stopped roaring as the plane rolled to a halt. There was a loud 'Bing!' as the 'fasten seat belts' sign went out.

"On behalf of the captain and crew we'd like to thank you for flying with Oceanic Airlines." 15

Pim opened the overhead locker and pulled out his enormous rucksack. The bag next to Pim's moved forward.

"Ow!" The passenger behind the kids cried out as the other bag fell on him. 20

"Oops. Sorry," said Pim.

10 **flight attendant** [ˈflaɪt əˌtendənt] Flugbegleiter/-in • 10 **intercom** [ˈɪntəkɒm] Sprechanlage • 14 **on behalf of** [ɒn bɪˈhɑːf ɒv] im Namen von • 15 **Oceanic** [əʊʃiˈænik]

"Going on to Adelaide, are you?" The man asked as he held his head.

"No. We're going to Argyle Downs. It's a cattle station in the outback," Pim replied.

5 "Good," the man said as he got up from his seat. The kids saw his trousers were dirty from the drinks which had spilled each time Pim had moved his seat. "With a larrikin like you out of the way, the rest of us can get a bit of peace and quiet."

10 A final announcement came over the intercom, "Would the De Groot family please make themselves known to a member of the cabin crew."

Jake, Maritska and Pim took their bags and pushed past the other passengers.

15 "We're the De Groots," Jake said to the male flight attendant near the exit.

"Your parents arranged for someone to take you to your connecting flight." The steward signalled to a young woman who was waiting at the gangway.

20 "Hi, I'm Alison." The woman walked up to them. She gave the kids a dazzling smile. "Follow me."

A wave of hot air swept over the kids as they stepped off the air conditioned plane.

"Oh, look!" cried Maritska as they walked into the
25 airport. She saw duty free shops on the other side. "They have Clinique. And Calvin Klein!"

Pim played around with his mobile phone. "I've got a signal! It has logged on to the network," he shouted happily.

30 Instinctively Maritska and Jake switched on their phones. "Mine hasn't," said Maritska. "How about yours?"

Jake checked his phone. "Nothing."

"Did you set up international roaming before you left?" asked Pim smugly.

---

3 **Argyle Downs** [ɑːˈgaɪl daʊnz] *Rinderfarm* • 3 **cattle station** [ˈkætl steɪʃn] Rinderfarm • 21 **dazzling** [ˈdæzlɪŋ] strahlend • 22 **to sweep** [swiːp] fegen • 30 **to switch sth on** [swɪtʃ] etw. einschalten • 34 **smug** [smʌg] selbstzufrieden

Maritska and Jake shook their heads.

"I did." Pim smirked.

"Techno geek," said Maritska jealously.

"You guys need to clear immigration," Alison carried on. "I can't come with you because of security. Once they've stamped your passports, follow the signs to baggage claim." 5

"Won't our bags be taken to our connecting flight?" asked Jake.

"Your next flight is from a different airport." Alison focussed her attention on Jake. "After you've collected your bags and gone through customs, follow the exit signs. Turn left at the yellow car hire desk. Walk fifty metres. Turn right at the blue taxi sign. I'll be waiting at the doors to the car park. Got that?" 10 15

Jake thought he remembered the directions. He didn't want to look stupid, so he nodded.

"What's a larrikin?" asked Pim as he fished his passport out of his rucksack.

"It's Aussie slang for a badly behaved kid. Why do you ask?" replied Alison. 20

"It's what a man on the plane called Pim," answered Maritska.

Alison tried not to laugh and told Pim strictly, "Behave yourself. I don't want you sent back home for being cheeky." Alison pointed them towards the immigration department's booths. "See you on the other side," she said as she left them on their own. 25

The lady on the desk scanned their passports, stamped them and waved the kids through with a friendly, "Welcome to Australia!" 30

It didn't take the kids long to find the baggage claim and collect their bags. Jake put them onto a trolley.

"I want to push it!" said Pim.

---

2 **to smirk** [smɜːk] feixen, hämisch grinsen • 3 **geek** [giːk] Freak • 6 **to stamp** [stæmp] stempeln • 6 **baggage claim** [ˈbæɡɪdʒ ˌkleɪm] Gepäckausgabe • 26 **cheeky** [ˈtʃiːki] frech • 27 **booth** [buːθ] Kabine • 33 **trolley** [ˈtrɒli] Gepäckkuli

Jake wasn't in the mood for an argument, so he let Pim take the trolley. "OK. But watch where you're going."

"Ow!" Jake heard a man cry out. He turned round to see Pim wheel the trolley over a man's foot. It was the same
5 man who had sat behind them on the plane.

"Sorry!" said Pim brightly. The man looked at the kids angrily as they walked off and disappeared through the customs barrier.

"OK, which way now?" Maritska asked Jake after the
10 last set of sliding doors closed behind them. They found themselves among many other travellers in the terminal.

"Umm," Jake looked around. There were so many people coming and going. It was really noisy. He tried hard to remember Alison's directions.

15 Jake was relieved to spot the car hire desk. "We turn right at the yellow desk."

"You sure?" Pim began to reply, "I don't think so, I think we should go –"

Jake cut him off. "I'm not stupid. I know which way to
20 go," Jake replied. "I'll push the trolley. Follow me. And keep up!" Jake took control and walked confidently through the airport. Pim and Maritska trailed behind.

"I told you. We're going into the airport, not out of it," Pim said as they came up to a bank of ATMs and Foreign
25 Exchange desks.

"Where's the taxi sign?" Jake's eyes searched left and right.

"Kids! Where do you think you're going?"

They turned round to find Alison running towards them.
30 "You were going in the wrong direction! Lucky I saw you before you got totally lost. Didn't you turn left at the yellow desk?" asked Alison.

---

13 **noisy** ['nɔɪzi] laut • 15 **relieved** [rɪ'liːvd] erleichtert • 15 **to spot** [spɒt] entdecken • 24 **bank** [bæŋk] *hier:* Reihe • 24 **ATM** [ˌeɪtiː'em] Geldautomat

"Stupid Jake turned right," said Maritska angrily. "We've only been in Australia for five minutes and he's got us lost."

"We should never follow you, Jake," Pim joined in. "You always get things wrong." 5

Maritska and Pim snickered with each other.

"No worries," said Alison brightly. She took the trolley from Jake and led the way to the car park.

Jake's cheeks burned with embarrassment. He was angry he had made another mistake the others could 10 tease him about.

Jake's mood darkened as they walked outside into the humid air and dazzling sunlight of the Darwin morning.

Jake had hoped the family's move to Australia would bring them closer together. But it seemed like things were 15 going to be just as difficult between them as they had been back home in Holland.

Chapter 2   Clouds on the horizon

As soon as they got into Alison's minivan, Pim phoned their parents to let them know they had arrived safely. Maritska and Pim sat up front with Alison. Jake sat quietly 20 in the back. He still felt stupid about losing his way at the airport.

"Yeah, yeah, we're all fine. The flight was cool." Pim held his phone in the air. "Say hi to Mum and Dad!"

Maritska and Jake shouted a greeting. 25

"OK. I know. See you soon." Pim switched his phone off.

"How come I didn't get to speak to them?" asked Maritska.

6 **to snicker** ['snɪkə] kichern • 9 **cheek** [tʃiːk] Wange • 10 **tease sb** [tiːz] sich über jmdn. lustig machen • 13 **humid** ['hjuːmɪd] feucht

"They said phone calls are very expensive over here," replied Pim.

Jake remembered how furious his parents had been when Pim had used his mobile phone to call them in America. They had received a huge bill so they had told Jake to make sure Pim was more careful with his phone in the future.

"Here we are," said Alison.

She pulled off the road and drove towards a group of low buildings. An orange windsock was blowing in the wind in the distance. Small planes were dotted around a large, flat airfield.

"Is this it?" asked Maritska. "It doesn't look much like an airport."

"Well it's small. But it's busy." Alison smiled. "Most of the cattle stations fly their workers in and out of this place. It's also a base for the flying vets and flying doctors. Oh, and the flying teachers fly in and out of here too."

"Does everyone fly in this country?" asked Pim.

"The Northern Territory of Australia is a big place. It'd take over a day to drive to Argyle Downs. And you'd have a pretty difficult journey since no road goes all the way there!" replied Alison.

The kids climbed out of the van. They stood together and narrowed their eyes in the strong sunlight.

A man suddenly ran out of one of the buildings. He wore beige shorts and a shirt. A wide-brimmed hat shielded his eyes from the sun. As he got closer they saw that he looked about sixty years old, but his energy and strong legs seemed as if they belonged to a much younger man.

"G'day!" The man held out his hand in welcome. "Don't say a word. Your parents talk about you all day long." The man studied the kids carefully. "Long blonde hair, a bit of a princess, but pretty as a picture. You must be Maritska."

10 **to blow** [bləʊ] wehen • 11 **to dot** [dɒt] übersäen, sprenkeln • 27 **wide-brimmed** [ˈwaɪd brɪmd] weitkrempig • 27 **to shield** [ʃiːld] abschirmen • 31 **G'day** *(Aust.)* [gəˈdaɪ] Guten Tag!

Maritska was a little offended by the 'princess' comment, but smiled proudly at the mention of her looks.

"Hair the colour of carrots, full of energy and a computer geek. You must be young Pim." The man ruffled Pim's hair. 5

Then he turned to Jake. "Curly black hair, dark serious eyes and someone you could trust your life with. You must be Jake."

Jake smiled happily. He was proud that his parents described him like that. 10

"But a terrible sense of direction," the man laughed.

Jake's smile disappeared at once. Maritska and Pim joined in the fun at his expense.

"Still, you can't have it all," said the man and slapped Jake on the shoulder. "I know all about you lot, but you 15 don't know anything about me yet. I'm Raymond Cooper Argyle, proud owner of Argyle Downs cattle station and pilot for the last part of your journey. Call me Ray!"

Ray and Alison quickly unloaded the kids' bags. Ray winced as he heaved Pim's rucksack onto the plane. "What 20 have you got in here, gold bars?"

"It's my laptop, my iPod, my Nintendo and my Playstation," replied Pim.

"Crikey," said Ray and rubbed his left shoulder. "It's a pity we haven't got any electricity at the ranch." 25

"What?!" Pim's eyes opened wide in horror.

Ray laughed. "Just joking."

Now Jake enjoyed a laugh at Pim's expense.

Ray carried on, "Of course we've got power. Your mum and dad couldn't do their scientific work in the dark. What 30 do they call it? 'Industrial biology'. Whatever it is, they've helped breed a new sort of cow. They give more milk, eat less grass and don't get sick. When this new herd arrives at

---

4 **to ruffle sth** ['rʌfl] etw. zerzausen • 7 **to trust sb with sth** [trʌst] jmdm. etw. anvertrauen • 13 **expense** [ɪk'spens] Kosten • 14 **to slap** [slæp] klopfen, schlagen • 20 **to wince** [wɪns] zusammenzucken • 21 **bar** [bɑː] *hier:* Barren • 24 **Crikey!** *(coll)* ['kraɪki] Meine Güte! • 32 **to breed** [briːd] züchten

the cattle auction I'll see the dollars roll in. If some thieves don't steal the money first, that is."

"I heard about the robbery on the TV news," said Alison.

5 "A couple of men with guns held up the auction last night," Ray told the kids. "They got away with over a million dollars in cash."

"I never realized there'd be so much money at a cattle auction," said Alison.

10 Ray chuckled. "People get rich from cattle sales in Australia. They used to make money from mining out here. There were tin and opal mines left, right and centre. Then they all ran dry. Luckily we've still got cows."

Maritska watched nervously as Ray put their bags on the 15 plane. It was really small. It had a single propeller at the front and only four seats inside. "How long is the flight?" she asked and gave a small cough.

"About three or four hours depending on the weather," replied Ray. He noticed the kids studying the plane. "Now 20 you can see why there wasn't room to bring your mum and dad to meet you." Ray threw their last bags in the back, closed the door and slapped the plane's side. "Hop on. You're up front with me," he told Jake. "The little ones in the back."

25 "But I want to sit in the front!" shouted Pim.

Ray shook his head. "In a light aircraft like this it's important to balance the weight. If you want to leave your computer stuff behind then you can ride up front."

"OK. I'll sit in the back," said Pim. The thought of not 30 having his games and computers really upset him.

Ray chuckled as he helped Pim into the plane. He rubbed his right arm, "Good. I wouldn't want to unload your bags. I almost pulled a muscle getting them on board!"

Alison watched the other kids climb into the plane. Its 35 single propeller began to spin and the wind from it blew

---

3 **robbery** ['rɒbri] Raubüberfall • 10 **to chuckle** ['tʃʌkl] kichern, in sich hinein lachen • 30 **to upset sb** ['ʌpset] jmdn. mitnehmen/aufregen

her dark hair around her face. "Bye, kids! Have a safe trip!" she shouted.

Inside the plane Jake tightened his seat belt. He watched Ray concentrate as he flicked switches and slipped on a headset. Jake looked over his shoulder. Pim and Maritska sat down in the back seats. Pim was playing around with his mobile phone while Maritska nervously chewed her hair. "Turn off your phone, you'll have no battery left. I don't think you should have it on in the plane anyway," Jake told Pim. Then he turned to Maritska. "And Mum says chewing your hair is really bad behaviour."

"This phone's battery lasts for days," replied Pim. "And I'm not calling anyone. I'm just playing a game." Pim carried on what he was doing.

"And if you don't tell Mum, then she won't know what I'm doing, will she?" Maritska said to Jake angrily and continued to chew her hair.

"Victor Hotel Whisky Tango Golf to tower. Request permission for takeoff. Over," Ray said into the microphone.

"Runway clear for takeoff. Over," came a quiet reply over his headset.

The kids turned round in their seats and waved goodbye to Alison. Their small plane rolled forward. It paused for a moment. The propeller suddenly began to spin much faster. The plane accelerated and sped along the runway. A few minutes later they were high up in the sky.

Darwin shimmered in the heat to their north. Ray's plane turned to the right and the city slipped away. Jake saw an endless area of land open up in front of them.

"Quite something, this country!" shouted Ray over the noise of the propeller. "A few hours' drive out of the city and you're in the desert. A young couple in a camper-van

---

4 to flick sth [flɪk] etw. betätigen/umlegen • 4 switch [swɪtʃ] Schalter • 7 to chew [tʃuː] kauen • 12 to last [lɑːst] *hier:* halten • 18 to request sth [rɪˈkwest] etw. erbitten • 19 permission [pəˈmɪʃn] Erlaubnis • 26 to accelerate [əkˈseləreɪt] beschleunigen • 28 heat [hiːt] Hitze • 33 camper-van [ˈkæmpə ˌvæn] Wohnwagen

got in trouble down there a few years ago. They had gone off the road and their van broke down. The police found them a couple of days later. It turned out they were only a few miles off the highway."

5 "Were they OK?" asked Maritska nervously.

Ray sadly shook his head. "Dead as doornails. They didn't have any food or water and it was hot. The only people who can survive those conditions in the wilderness are the Aborigines. One of the workers on my ranch took

10 off without a word last year. He came back six months later. He had walked to Alice Springs and back. Said he needed to see a mate!"

"He walked there and back?" asked Jake.

"Those guys do it all the time," nodded Ray, "and without

15 maps. They know which way to go by the songs they sing. They tell them where the waterholes are, the best places to find bush tucker and the like."

The kids looked puzzled.

"'Tucker' is the Aussie word for food. Wallabies, dingoes,

20 roos. They know how to track them and hunt them. They know which grubs and ants you can eat and which will poison you," explained Ray. "That's what we call 'bush tucker.'"

Pim started talking excitedly about eating disgusting

25 things. Maritska was shocked by the idea of eating insects. This made Pim imagine even more awful things to eat.

The kids in the back teased each other and laughed as Ray told more of his stories. Jake watched the land below them change. Every so often there was a small town or a

30 station. Then Jake realized they had flown for an hour and he hadn't seen a single building or road.

He noticed that Ray had gone very quiet. He followed Ray's eyes. Thick clouds had suddenly blown up in front of them. They had come out of nowhere.

---

6 **dead as doornails** [ˌded æz ˈdɔːneɪlz] mausetot • 8 **condition** [kənˈdɪʃn] Bedingung • 18 **puzzled** [ˈpʌzld] verwirrt • 22 **to poison** [ˈpɔɪzn] vergiften • 24 **disgusting** [dɪsˈɡʌstɪŋ] ekelhaft

"Buckle up, kids," said Ray firmly. "It's gonna get bumpy."

Jake tightened his seat belt. Ray turned sharply to the right. But before the plane could turn, it was suddenly in the middle of the clouds.

Maritska screamed as the plane shook violently. There was a loud rattle and it was like someone had thrown brown sand across the windscreen. Everywhere around the plane there were clouds of red sand. Ray switched on the windscreen wipers.

"What is it?" shouted Jake.

"A sandstorm!" Ray called out. "Wasn't on the forecast. No worries. We can go round it."

Ray pulled back the throttle. The plane climbed, but the shaking got worse. Ray moved the throttle to the left. He had to fight really hard to control the plane. Suddenly he let out a cry of pain. His right hand dropped from the controls. The plane's nose went down.

"We're going down!" screamed Maritska.

The plane quickly plunged towards the ground.

1 **to buckle up** ['bʌkl] sich anschnallen • 1 **firm** [fɜːm] fest, bestimmt •
8 **windscreen** ['wɪndskriːn] Windschutzscheibe • 10 **windscreen wiper**
['wɪndskriːn ˌwaɪpə] Scheibenwischer • 14 **throttle** ['θrɒtl] Steuerknüppel •
20 **to plunge** ['plʌndʒ] stürzen

"Help me pull her up," gasped Ray.

Jake was scared, but had no choice. He reached across and grabbed the right side of the throttle with both hands.

With Ray using his good hand on the other side, the two
5 of them managed to pull the throttle back. It took all of Jake's strength to fight their fall. After what felt like hours, the plane slowly began to climb.

With a final rattle and shake, the plane reappeared from the cloud. The windscreen wipers cleared the windscreen
10 and they saw blue sky again.

"Phew," said Pim. "That was great!"

Jake took his trembling hands off the throttle. But he wasn't as relieved as Pim. Ray's face had gone deathly white. There was sweat on his forehead. Ray was trying to
15 use both hands on the controls but he was having difficulty moving his right arm.

Ray jiggled his headset. "Does anyone read me? Over," he shouted into the microphone. There was no reply. "Kids, I'm sick. I have to land," he croaked.

20 "Here?" cried Maritska. Some of the sand had blown off the windows. The kids saw they were in the middle of nowhere. "Why can't we carry on?"

"Something is up with my heart," gasped Ray and held his chest.

25 Jake turned to Maritska and Pim, "I think he's had a heart attack."

"What? What?!" Maritska's eyes were wide with terror.

Jake remembered the safety card from the big plane. He shouted back to Pim and Maritska. "Put your heads
30 on your knees! Place your hands over your head! Brace yourselves!"

In spite of his pain Ray tried hard to keep the plane under control. The ground got closer. The wheels narrowly missed a rock.

---

6 **strengh** [ˈstreŋθ] Kraft • 12 **to tremble** [ˈtrembl] zittern • 14 **forehead** [ˈfɒrɪd] Stirn • 17 **to jiggle** [ˈdʒɪɡl] wackeln, rütteln • 19 **to croak** [krəʊk] krächzen • 24 **chest** [tʃest] Brust • 30 **to brace oneself** [breɪs] sich abstützen/vorbereiten

"Mayday. Mayday," Ray gasped into the microphone. He fell forward on the throttle. The plane's nose sank to the ground.

Jake pushed Ray away from the controls. He grabbed the throttle and pulled it back. The nose lifted a little, just enough to stop them from immediately crashing. 5

"What do I do?" shouted Jake. "Ray!"

Ray's eyes flickered. With an enormous effort he took the controls with his left hand. The plane's propeller slowed. Jake saw an area of smooth land up ahead. 10

Ray guided the plane towards it. The wheels brushed the sand. The plane rattled violently. There was a loud 'Bang!' as the plane's tail hit the ground.

The plane rose into the air a little as Ray tried hard to keep it under control. 15

Maritska screamed hysterically.

"We're going to crash!" Pim cried.

"Keep your heads down!" shouted Jake. He was afraid they were about to die. He didn't want his brother and sister to see their plane crash into the sand and rocks. 20

There was a series of loud cracks. Jake turned round and saw the plane's tail rip off and fall away. The bags in the back flew out and fell to the ground. Only centimetres more and Pim and Maritska's seats would have been ripped out, too. Wind blew through the cabin from the open hole. 25

"Stay near the plane. You'll be OK." Ray's eyes dropped shut and his head fell onto his chest.

The plane hit the earth and slid across the ground.

Jake leaned forward and pressed his face onto his knees, held his head and shut his eyes. He knew what was about 30 to happen to them would be horrible; he just hoped that it would be over with quickly.

---

6 **immediately** [ɪˈmiːdiətli] sofort • 8 **to flicker** [ˈflɪkə] zucken, flackern • 8 **effort** [ˈefət] Anstrengung • 11 **to brush** [brʌʃ] *hier:* streifen • 13 **tail** [teɪl] hinteres Ende, Schwanz • 22 **to rip off** [ˈrɪp ɒf] abreißen

Chapter 3   Good news and bad news

After what felt like an eternity of rocking, and a very loud roar, the plane came to a halt.

Jake stayed in the brace position. He was afraid to lift his head. Then he heard Maritska crying softly in the back and
5 Pim say, "We're OK."

Relieved that both of them were still alive, Jake finally opened his eyes and sat up.

Ray had managed to fly the plane towards a large, soft bank of sand. Amazingly, this had slowed them down
10 enough to stop the plane from totally breaking into pieces.

Jake shook Ray, but there was no answer. The man was clearly dead.

"Take his headset," said Pim. "Call for help."

Jake gently took the headphones off Ray and put them
15 on.

"Can anyone hear me?" Jake said into the microphone. He couldn't hear anything in the ear phones – only the buzz of static. Jake played around with the switch he had seen Ray use to contact the tower.

20 "I smell something weird," said Maritska.

Jake and Pim smelled the air.

Jake knew immediately it was petrol. The smallest spark could make the plane explode. "We have to get out. Now!" Jake ripped off the headset and flipped open his seat belt.
25 He managed to quickly kick open his door and jump from the plane. As he reached back to help Maritska, he saw petrol running out from the other side of the plane.

"Pim! This way. Get out on my side," Jake shouted.

Pim's face disappeared behind the seat. "I dropped my
30 phone," Pim searched for it on the floor at the back.

"Leave it," Jake ordered.

---

1 **eternity** [ɪˈtɜːnəti] Ewigkeit • 19 **static** [ˈstætɪk] statische Elektrizität • 23 **petrol** [ˈpetrl] Benzin • 23 **spark** [spɑːk] Funke

Pim ignored Jake, he kept on looking.

Jake ran round to the back of the plane. There was a giant hole where the tail had been torn away.

"I think I see it," Pim muttered and his head disappeared below the seat. ⁵

Jake leant inside and grabbed hold of Pim.

"Leave off," shouted Pim as he wriggled away from Jake. "I need my –"

Jake didn't take any notice of Pim. He pulled him out of the plane and dragged him away from it. ¹⁰

Maritska ran after them as Pim tried hard to free himself. "Why did you do that, Jake?" she shouted. "You should have let him look –"

A huge explosion threw them all to the ground.

After a moment the three of them looked up and saw ¹⁵ the wreck of the plane in a ball of flames.

"He said to stay with the plane," said Maritska as she shielded her eyes from the sun.

"We have to find shade. Remember that couple in the camper-van who cooked in the heat?" replied Jake. ²⁰

4 **to mutter** ['mʌtə] murmeln • 10 **to drag sb** [dræg] jmdn. zerren • 16 **wreck** [rek] Wrack • 19 **shade** [ʃeɪd] Schatten

"This is terrible," cried Maritska. She looked around. They were in the middle of a red desert. There was a huge rock in the distance to their left. A few trees and bushes were dotted along the horizon. The burning sun was almost directly overhead. There were no shadows, so they had no idea of east or west. Maritska suddenly jumped to her feet. "I see my bag!" she shouted.

Jake couldn't believe that at a time like this she was interested in her clothes and make-up. But once she had rescued her bag from where it had fallen off the plane, Jake had to admit she wasn't so crazy.

"Here." Maritska pulled out some baseball caps and a wide-brimmed hat. She put on the hat, handed one cap to Jake and one to Pim.

"I'm not wearing pink," Pim said.

"Put it on," Jake told him. "Or you'll get a sunstroke."

Reluctantly, Pim pulled on the cap. Jake turned his cap round to keep the sun off the back of his neck.

"Do you think anyone heard the call on the radio?" asked Maritska.

"No worries," said Pim imitating Ray's Aussie accent. "Luckily, I found this before you pulled me out of the plane!" He waved his mobile phone. "It's 3G. And it has got GPS. I was getting a signal a while back. All we need to do is call Mum and Dad for help or find a map to show us where we are."

Jake and Maritska sighed with relief. Happy, for once, that Pim was such a techno geek.

Pim dialled and pressed the 'call' button. The smile on his face disappeared. He tried again. "Oh, no," he said.

Jake and Maritska leaned forward. "What?!"

Pim hung his head, "The battery is dead."

"I told you to turn it off!" shouted Jake.

---

5 **shadow** [ˈʃædəʊ] Schatten • 16 **sunstroke** [ˈsʌnstrəʊk] Sonnenstich •
17 **reluctant** [rɪˈlʌktnt] widerwillig • 27 **to sigh** [sai] seufzen • 29 **to dial**
[daiəl] wählen

"You idiot!" screamed Maritska. "If you hadn't been playing around and wasting the battery, we'd be OK."

"I didn't know. Stop blaming me. I'm only a little kid." Pim hung his head.

Maritska looked at the black smoke rising from the ⁵ crashed plane. "Maybe someone will see the smoke?"

"When we don't arrive, Mum and Dad will come and look for us. We just have to wait," said Jake.

"I'm thirsty," complained Pim.

Jake checked his watch. It was just after two o'clock in ¹⁰ the afternoon. He realized they had had nothing to eat since breakfast on the plane. "I think we should head for those trees." Jake pointed to the horizon.

"We should stay near the plane," said Maritska.

"It's the middle of the day. We must get out of the sun," ¹⁵ said Jake.

Maritska reluctantly agreed and picked up her bag.

The kids began to walk. The sand was so hot they could feel it burning through their shoes. Jake's lips were dry. He realized that without water they'd be in trouble pretty ²⁰ soon. But right now he was grateful for one thing – they were all alive and unhurt.

Chapter 4   Cries in the wilderness

Minutes felt like hours as the kids sat under the trees and watched the sun slip across the sky.

Jake stared into the distance. Shadows formed on the ²⁵ big rock as the sun started to go down. "At least now we know which way is west," Jake said watching the sunset.

Maritska got up and wandered around the trees. "I think someone was here before." She pointed to strange

---

3 **to blame sb** [bleɪm] jmdm. die Schuld geben • 9 **to be thirsty** [ˈθɜːsti] Durst haben • 19 **lip** [lɪp] Lippe • 21 **grateful** [ˈɡreɪtfʊl] dankbar

criss-cross patterns on the earth. "It's like someone has been drawing in the sand."

"Why would anyone come here to draw in the sand? You're stupid," said Pim. They had found Jake's bag and Pim's computer bag as they walked to the trees. Although it was extremely heavy, Pim had insisted on taking the bag with him. Now he kept playing with the laptop's keyboard in the hope it might come to life.

Jake saw the trail of a large passenger jet cut across the sky.

Maritska ran from under the trees and waved her hands in the air. "Maybe they'll see us," she said hopefully.

"Maybe," replied Jake. He was certain they wouldn't.

Every so often they heard odd sounds. Birds rattled through the branches overhead. Some animals howled. They sounded like dogs. Crickets and lizards made strange sounds in the distance.

"It's getting dark," cried Maritska. "I'm so tired."

"We'll have to sleep here," said Jake.

The sun was sinking fast. The trees made long shadows across the sand.

"This sucks," moaned Pim. "I'm thirsty. And hungry." Jake's stomach was rumbling, too. He could hardly keep his eyes open. They'd been travelling for nearly two days without a good night's sleep. And jet lag was kicking in, too.

The sun disappeared behind the big rock. Night fell almost at once.

"I can't spend the night here. I want to go home. Help! Someone, help us!" Maritska shouted in the darkness. Her fear upset Pim. He ran to his sister and stood next to her. "Help!" he shouted with her. "Help us! Please!"

---

1 **criss-cross pattern** ['krɪskrɒs ˌpætn] kreuz und quer verlaufendes Muster •
6 **to insist on sth** [ɪnˈsɪst] auf etw. bestehen • 15 **branch** [brɑːnʃ] Zweig • 15 **to howl** [haʊl] heulen • 16 **lizard** [ˈlɪzəd] Eidechse • 22 **This sucks!** [ˌðɪs ˈsʌks] Zum Kotzen! • 23 **to rumble** [ˈrʌmbl] *hier:* knurren

Maritska and Pim's cries died away. The howls of the dingoes in the distance grew louder, as if in reply.

"I hear something," Maritska suddenly said. She was shaking and told them all to be really quiet.

They stood in silence. They couldn't see anyone, but they heard the soft sound of footsteps in the sand. 5

"Don't move ..." came a voice from the darkness.

The kids froze in terror.

There was a whizzing sound. A white stick flew past their faces. It disappeared into the darkness and landed in the sand with a thud. 10

Jake turned round.

A figure appeared. The moon had risen and its pale light reflected off the dark skin of the person coming towards them. 15

"Stay still," said the figure.

At first Jake thought it was a boy. But as the figure walked past them he saw it was a girl. She had thick, wavy black hair, was dressed in a bikini made of brown animal skins and carried a pack of white sticks on her back. 20

8 **to freeze** [friːz] *hier:* erstarren • 9 **to whizz** [wɪz] flitzen • 11 **thud** [θʌd] dumpfer Schlag • 13 **pale** [peɪl] blass

Maritska and Pim held on to each other in fear. Part of them was relieved to see another person, but another part was scared of this strange being.

"Nice," they heard the girl say in the darkness.

5 "Who are you?" shouted Jake. "Can you help us?"

The girl came back to them. She held a giant snake in her hands. The white stick which had shot past them stuck out of its dead body.

"I already have," she said and smiled. Her white teeth
10 and sparkling eyes shone in the moonlight. She held the snake out to them, "I just saved your lives."

Chapter 5   Marks on the earth

Maritska stared in horror at the dead snake.

The girl pointed to the marks in the sand which Maritska had thought were drawings. "That's how you tell when
15 snakes are around. If this had bit you, pretty soon you'd be dead."

Jake shuddered. If they had gone to sleep there, it was likely they'd never have woken up.

"We've got food now too," she said and took out her
20 knife.

"Eat that?" asked Maritska.

"If its bite can kill, how can we eat it?" asked Pim.

In one quick move the girl cut off the snake's head. They looked at it in horror. The girl saw their disgust. She hid
25 the head behind her back. Then she quickly brought it back and waved the dead head at them.

Pim and Maritska jumped back because they didn't want any blood to drip on them.

---

6 **snake** [sneɪk] Schlange • 10 **to sparkle** ['spɑːkl] funkeln • 13 **mark** [mɑːk] Spur •
15 **to bite** [baɪt] beißen • 17 **to shudder** ['ʃʌdə] schaudern • 24 **disgust** [dɪsˈgʌst]
Ekel • 28 **to drip** [drɪp] tropfen

The girl laughed. "The poison sacks are up here. The rest of it is good to eat."

Jake smiled; it was fun to see someone tease Pim and Maritska for a change. "Who are you?" Jake asked the girl.

"I'm Kyeema," she answered. She was busy collecting 5 sticks and piling them up.

"Wow. Are you going to show us some magical way to make fire?" asked Pim.

Kyeema's eyes opened wide. "Yes. Very mysterious. I make fire with a gift from my ancestors. Watch closely." 10

The kids leaned forward, eager to see how she was going to do it.

Kyeema reached into the pack with her spears. She whipped out a small, red plastic object. She flicked it open and a flame shot out. "It's called a lighter," she said and set 15 fire to the sticks.

It didn't take long for the fire to take hold. The kids sat around it and watched Kyeema cook the snake. She gave the first piece to Jake. Not wanting to look like a wimp, he took a big bite. 20

"Is it OK?" asked Pim.

"I'd prefer a Big Mac, but it's not bad," said Jake.

Kyeema gave Pim a piece of snake. He made a face as he ate it, but he was so hungry he was glad for anything.

Maritska only tried a little bit of hers. "It's disgusting. I 25 can't eat this," she said and put her piece of snake meat down.

Kyeema shrugged. "No worries, all the more for us."

After they had eaten, Kyeema said she'd find them some water. She hacked a branch off the tree and set the end 30 on fire. She walked forward, bent down and stared at the sand.

"What are you looking for?" asked Jake.

---

5 **Kyeema** [kaɪˈiːmɑː] Speer • 13 **spear** [spɪə] Speer • 15 **lighter** [ˈlaɪtə] Feuerzeug • 19 **wimp** [wɪmp] Waschlappen, Angsthase • 31 **to bend down** [bɛnd ˈdaʊn] sich bücken

"Animal tracks," she replied. "See," she pointed to small dents in the sand. "Dingoes. All we have to do is follow where they went."

The moon was bright and, away from the fire, the kids'
5 eyes got used to the dark. They could see the animals' tracks quite clearly.

They only had to walk for ten minutes or so before they reached a small valley surrounded by grass. In its middle, the moon reflected in a pool of water.

10 Pim and Maritska ran down to it happily.

"Is it good to drink?" asked Jake.

"If it's good enough for dingoes and roos, it's good enough for us," said Kyeema and ran after the kids.

"How come this is here?" asked Pim as he drank water
15 from his clasped hands.

"The rain fills all the low parts. This will dry up soon," Kyeema explained. "Then the animals go somewhere else."

After they had drunk all they needed, the kids made
20 their way back to the trees. Kyeema threw more sticks on the fire.

Pim and Maritska were so tired, now that they had had something to drink, that they fell asleep within seconds.

Jake and Kyeema stayed awake and stared into the
25 flames. They told each other how they had ended up here.

"You're from Holland?" asked Kyeema. "If you're Dutch, how come you speak English so well?"

Jake explained that his family had lived all over Europe because of his parents' work. Between them the kids spoke
30 four languages and could argue fluently in all of them.

Kyeema wondered why Jake and his brother and sister looked so different from one another.

---

2 dent [dent] Vertiefung • 8 valley ['vælɪ] Tal • 8 surrounded by [sə'raʊndɪd baɪ] umgeben von • 15 to clasp [kla:sp] *hier:* zusammendrücken • 24 awake ['əweɪk] wach

"I'm adopted," he said. "And Pim and Maritska are half brother and sister. I joined the family when they were young. Our parents gave me the biggest bedroom and they've hated me ever since."

Kyeema's parents were dead, too, and she had been living with her sister. She told him about the settlement where her people, the Yolngu tribe, lived. She told him about the conflict between their old ways and the modern world. The government believed Aboriginal kids were missing out on education and work opportunities. Some of Kyeema's friends had been sent to live with white families a long way away in the hope it would improve their futures.

Kyeema had always wanted to discover more about the world. But she didn't want to be sent to the city before she had experienced all she could in the outback. She had decided to go and try out for herself the things she had learned by watching the older members of her tribe. She decided to go on a walkabout.

"I thought only boys did that," said Jake.

Kyeema immediately flew into a rage. "You sound like them! The old ones don't like change. I can do anything a boy can! I hunt. I follow tracks. I know most of the words to the songs. I have the right to prove myself as much as a boy. What should I have done? Sat at home and waited for some guy to come along and marry me?"

Jake raised his hands in defence, "Sorry. I didn't mean to be rude."

Kyeema shook her head. "You're all right, mate. This gets me mad sometimes. Our people have got a lot of history. But I've never wanted to live in the past. I've always wanted to learn from the past so I could build up my own future!"

"Whatever the reason, I'm glad you decided to go on a walkabout," Jake said. "Lucky you came by when you did. If not, we'd probably be dead."

---

7 **Yolngu** ['jəʊlŋʊ] • 18 **walkabout** ['wɔːkəˌbaʊt] *rituelle Wanderung* • 20 **to fly into a rage** [ˌflaɪ ɪntə ə 'reɪdʒ] sich in Rage reden • 22 **to hunt** [hʌnt] jagen • 26 **defence** [dɪ'fens] Abwehr • 28 **all right** [ɔːl'raɪt] (schon) in Ordnung

Kyeema stared at Jake. "It wasn't luck, Dutch."

Their eyes met in the sparkling firelight.

"Paths cross for a reason," said Kyeema. She looked over to where Pim and Maritska slept under the trees. Jake
5 leant back and used his jacket as a pillow.

"How do you know which way to go?" he asked sleepily.

"Everything that happens in life leaves a mark in the world," said Kyeema. "There'll be a scar on the earth where your plane crashed. The tree will show a wound where I
10 cut off the branch. Those are recent things. Our songs tell stories from when the world came into being during the Dreamtime. You see that big rock on the horizon? That's where the lizard ancestor was buried after he died on his walk to the sea."

15 "But that's just a story."

"After our lives have ended, what's left but stories people tell about us? I want someone to tell a story about me one day. I want to make a mark on the world and change it for the better. I don't want to be forgotten. Get some sleep,
20 Dutch. We've got a big day tomorrow."

The fire crackled. Jake's eyes closed. Kyeema and the outback disappeared into blackness and he fell asleep.

Chapter 6   Kyeema's song

Jake had strange dreams. One minute he was on a plane, the next he was falling through the air. One second
25 everyone was congratulating him for doing something good and the next moment people were blaming him for doing something bad. For one second, just before he woke up, he dreamt his real mother and father were still alive.

---

1 **Dutch** [dʌtʃ] Holländer/-in • 8 **scar** [skɑː] Narbe • 9 **wound** [wuːnd] Wunde •
13 **to bury** ['berɪ] begraben • 21 **to crackle** ['krækl] knistern • 25 **to congratulate**
[kənˈɡrætʃʊleɪt] gratulieren

Jake opened his eyes and blinked. The sunlight was shining directly into his face. "Kyeema?" he sat up and looked around. They had all gone. Jake panicked. Where were Pim and Maritska? Suddenly he was scared that they had all run off and left him alone. 5

"Ow!" Jake cried out. Something hit him on the back of the head. He picked it up and saw it was a round, red fruit.

"Got ya!" he heard Pim shout.

"Good shot," came Kyeema's voice. Jake turned to find 10 Kyeema, Maritska and Pim running across the sand.

"Eat it fast. We've got to get moving," shouted Kyeema.

Jake bit into the fruit. It was a bit like a peach, with a hard stone in the middle.

"It's called a 'quandong,'" Pim said confidently. 15

"Fruits which are red are usually good to eat," said Kyeema. "You mustn't eat any yellow things. And any fruit which doesn't look good to eat probably isn't."

Maritska finished her quandong. She threw the stone away and picked up her bag. "I've had enough of this. Let's 20 go and get rescued."

Pim picked up his bag of computer stuff.

Kyeema stared at them like they were crazy. She shook her head gravely, "You must leave it all behind."

Maritska and Pim insisted they bring their things with 25 them.

"It took me years to save up for this," Pim said and held up his Playstation.

Maritska held her bag of clothes and make-up tightly.

"Which would you rather have," asked Kyeema, "your 30 life or your possessions?"

"I want both," replied Maritska.

Her honesty made Jake laugh. "Come on," he said. "See how Kyeema travels. She only has what she needs."

---

1 **to blink** [blɪŋk] blinzeln • 13 **peach** [piːtʃ] Pfirsich • 14 **stone** [stəʊn] Stein •
15 **quandong** [ˈkwɒndɒŋ] *essbare Frucht* • 24 **gravely** [ˈɡreɪvlɪ] ernst •
31 **possession** [pəˈzeʃn] Besitz • 33 **honesty** [ˈɒnɪstɪ] Ehrlichkeit

Jake pushed his bag to the side. It had his phone and all his clothes and books in it. "We can't carry this stuff with us."

Pim and Maritska knew Jake was right. Sadly they left their possessions behind.

5 Kyeema held her hand above her eyes and looked into the distance. Then, after closing her eyes for a moment, she began to sing quietly. After a couple of notes she began to walk.

Mystified, Jake, Pim and Maritska followed her.

• • •

10 They didn't understand the words of the song Kyeema sang. It was in her language and many of the words were secret. It would be wrong to teach them to someone who wasn't of her tribe. In fact, because she was a girl, there were some words nobody would ever teach her. This upset
15 her; it meant there'd always be some part of her history she'd never know. And just because she was a girl!

After they had walked for an hour or so Jake began to understand that there was a connection between the music of her song and the landscape. When the notes of
20 Kyeema's song were long and the same tone, then the land was flat and empty. If the notes got faster and higher, the land was uneven and high. If they were fast and low, the ground was uneven and low.

They passed the big rock, the one Kyeema called the
25 resting place of the lizard ancestor. It was on their left. The sun was nearing its high point in the sky and all the mysterious shadows on the rock disappeared.

Kyeema found a watering hole at the base of the rock and they drank. Pim was already hungry again. While they
30 were drinking, they suddenly heard some noises. They looked up to see two animals' faces above the rock.

"Sshh," said Kyeema putting her finger to her lips.

The kids stood still. The animals stared down at them.

---

9 **mystified** ['mɪstɪfaɪd] verblüfft • 22 **uneven** [ʌn'iːvn] uneben • 25 **resting place** ['restɪŋ ˌpleɪs] Ruhestätte

Jake thought they looked like dogs. They had sandy, red coloured fur, long pointed snouts and amber eyes. Their colouring was perfect in the desert. They blended in so well with the earth and rocks one could hardly see them.

"We should go," whispered Kyeema. "They're dingoes. 5 This is their place. Let them drink."

"My stomach is empty," moaned Pim. He tried to grab one of the spears from Kyeema's back. "You said I've got good aim. Let's kill one and eat it!"

"Leave them!" Kyeema took the spear from his hand and 10 pushed him away from the rocks. She was very angry. Pim looked scared. "Come!" she ordered. Kyeema marched off. After a moment the kids trailed after her.

Jake looked back. The dingoes stood on the lizard ancestor's rock and watched them leave. They didn't go to 15 drink. They just watched. Jake felt their eyes on him as he walked away.

Kyeema sang low and quiet and they could hardly hear her as she marched on ahead. After a while Jake ran to catch up with her. "I'm sorry. He shouldn't have tried to 20 take your spear without asking." He thought this was the reason she was upset.

"It would have been a bad thing if we had hurt them." Kyeema said. She explained that to allow a dingo to be killed would be the worst thing she could ever do. Her 25 people believed certain animals are your totem. For some it would be the golden ant. For others the emu. Their belief was that this totem animal watched over you and was sacred. So sacred, it would be wrong to even draw a picture of a dingo if it was your totem. 30

Jake understood now why hurting a dingo would have been so upsetting for her. He went back and tried to explain this to Pim.

---

2 **fur** [fɜ:] Fell • 2 **snout** [snaʊt] Schnauze • 2 **amber** ['æmbə] bernsteinfarben •
3 **to blend in** ['blend ɪn] sich optisch angleichen • 8 **to have good aim** [eɪm] gut
zielen können • 28 **belief** [bɪ'li:f] Glaube • 29 **sacred** ['seɪkrɪd] heilig

Pim didn't really understand, but he liked Kyeema and wanted to be friends with her again. He ran ahead and spoke to her. Pim and Kyeema exchanged words. Kyeema's anger faded. A moment later Pim said something which 5 made her laugh. She waved at Jake and Maritska.

"She's weird," muttered Maritska as they caught up, "she eats snakes and has terrible taste in clothes."

The group walked on for a few more hours, but the sun was getting high in the sky and they were in open ground. 10 Bright green and orange birds flew overhead. Then they turned and disappeared.

Kyeema signalled to the kids and they followed the birds.

In a deep dip in the land they found a small area of short 15 and thick trees and bushes around a watering hole. If they hadn't seen where the birds had gone, they would have missed it.

"That's why you must look at everything," explained Kyeema. "Really look. Do not miss a thing. If you ever 20 need food or water, follow the animals that live here."

They rested under the trees. Kyeema dug in a tree stump with a stick. It was full of witchetty grubs and ants. She picked up a wriggling grub and offered it to the kids. Pim ate it greedily and happily.

25 Maritska still didn't want to eat strange things. She kept on coughing. Jake thought it was a sign she was trying to hide how scared she really was.

Jake asked Kyeema about the songs she sang. She told them about her people's belief in the Dreamtime. This was 30 the period before living memory when spirits came out of the earth and down from the sky to create the land and all living things. The song she sang on this journey told of how the lizard ancestor crawled across the earth looking for the sea. Every part of the song spoke of something the

4 **anger** ['æŋgə] Ärger • 14 **dip** [dɪp] Senke • 21 **stump** [stʌmp] Stumpf •
24 **greedy** ['griːdi] gierig • 30 **living memory** [ˌlɪvɪŋ 'meməri] Menschengedenken
• 33 **to crawl** [krɔːl] kriechen

lizard had done that changed or created the landscape. The group of hills was where it had laid its eggs. A group of deep grooves were made when its babies crawled away. And the big rock was where the lizard lay down and died.

After a short rest they walked on. Kyeema said she couldn't teach them any of the sacred words of the song, but they could sing the melody. So they walked on and raised their voices, making up funny words to go with the music.

Even though they weren't singing the right words, Jake made a connection between the melody and the landscape. He saw the landmarks which Kyeema described in her song.

"Nearly there," said Kyeema.

They stopped and stared at a huge bank of rocks in front of them.

"What's on the other side?" asked Jake.

"You'll see," said Kyeema. She ran forward and sprinted over the boulders.

"Now we have to climb?" asked Maritska weakly. "What next?"

Pim started climbing over the rocks. Jake reached back and helped Maritska.

"This is crazy," Maritska moaned. "We've been walking all day. How much further do we have to go? Why is this stupid country so big? Back in Holland ..." Her words trailed off as they got to the top of the rocks.

"Ha!" cried Kyeema triumphantly.

They looked down and smiled at one another.

There, cutting through the outback, was a solid, tarmac road.

3 **groove** [gruːv] Furche • 19 **boulder** [ˈbəʊldə] Geröll • 30 **solid** [ˈsɒlɪd] fest • 30 **tarmac** [ˈtɑːmæk] Asphalt

Chapter 7   Bob and Jolene to the rescue

Pim and Maritska laughed with joy as they stumbled down the rocks. The road was empty, but at least it was a road. They knew it wouldn't take too long until someone drove by. In fact, a cloud of dust in the distance meant traffic was
5 already heading their way.

Jake smiled at Kyeema. "Your songlines seem as good as any map," he said. "I don't understand the conflict between your people and the modern world."

Kyeema pointed to Pim. He was already at the side of
10 the road jumping up and down with excitement. "When he's back in the city, he'll soon forget about the magic of this land. And your sister has no interest in the journey, only the destination." Kyeema stared at the dust on the horizon.

15 "I love modern things, too, but I value the knowledge you've taught me. Surely there's a way the old world and the new can live side by side?" asked Jake.

Kyeema looked doubtful as she followed Jake down the rocks towards the road.

20 "Believe one thing," he said to her, "I'll never forget you."

Kyeema shrugged. "Words are easy," she said, "it's the things we do which leave marks on the earth."

The car in the distance got closer. It was a white camper-
25 van, but it was covered by a thick layer of red dust.

Pim jumped up and down. "Hello!" he shouted and waved his arms. Maritska joined in. "Help!"

Jake was nearly at their side when Kyeema grabbed his arm. "Let it go," she whispered.

30 "We have to get help," said Jake. He couldn't understand why Kyeema would want them to miss their chance of rescue. He wondered if she didn't want their adventure to end just yet.

---

1 to stumble [ˈstʌmbl] stolpern • **4 dust** [dʌst] Staub • **13 destination** [ˌdestɪˈneɪʃn] Ziel • **17 doubtful** [ˈdaʊtfʊl] zweifelnd, skeptisch

"I've got a bad feeling about what's coming, Dutch." Kyeema's dark eyes were troubled as she watched the van get closer.

But Jake wouldn't listen. He walked away from her. "I have to think of Maritska and Pim," he said. "They need proper food and rest." Jake turned round to find Kyeema wasn't at his side anymore. "Kyeema?" he called out. Jake immediately remembered what she had taught him. He checked for her tracks to see which way she had gone. All he could make out were small dents like the tracks of a dingo. It was as if she had vanished into thin air.

The camper-van was very close to them and it showed no sign of slowing down.

"Can't they see us?" asked Maritska.

"Hey, hey!" screamed Pim.

The van was nearly on them.

Maritska was terrified the van might drive past and not pick them up. Jake held her arm, but she wriggled free and ran into the middle of the road. "Don't!" yelled Jake, but Pim followed her at once.

Jake couldn't bear to look as the van came to a halt. It stopped centimetres from Pim and Maritska's legs.

"Stupid idiots," roared a rough man's voice as the door opened. "You nearly got yourselves killed!"

The other door opened and a woman jumped out. "Oh my God, Bob! Were you driving with your eyes shut? Kids, are you OK?" The woman came towards them. She wore lots of turquoise necklaces and had a guitar hanging around her neck.

Maritska started crying. The woman took off her guitar and carefully put it in the van. She ran to Maritska and hugged her. She looked at the kids. They had dirty, sunburnt faces and ripped clothes. "What the hell happened to you guys?"

---

6 **proper** ['prɒpə] richtig, anständig • 11 **to vanish into thin air** ['vænɪʃ] sich in Luft auflösen • 23 **rough** [rʌf] rau • 28 **turquoise** ['tɜːkwɑːz] türkis • 28 **necklace** ['nekləs] Kette • 32 **to hug sb** [hʌg] umarmen

"Our plane crashed," said Pim.

"The man who was flying it died," Maritska blurted out. "We've walked all day to get here."

"You found your way across the outback by yourselves?" asked the man.

Jake's eyes ran along the horizon, searching for Kyeema. "Someone showed us the way," he said. "An Aboriginal girl."

The woman was concerned. "I don't see anyone. Where did she go?"

"I don't know," said Jake.

The woman looked at the man. "Funny to take off just like that." She turned her attention back to the kids, "Sounds like you guys were very lucky."

They saw another car in the distance, a shiny black Mercedes. The man looked at the car, then at his watch. "Can't hang around all day, Jolene," he said to the woman. "We said we'd make it to Doomadgee by sunset."

"We don't have to do everything according to a stupid timetable, Bob," said Jolene angrily. "You nearly ran these kids over because you were driving like a maniac!" Jolene guided Maritska towards the van, "The map says there's a gas station up ahead. We'll give you a lift there and you can call for help."

"Don't you have a phone we can use now?" asked Jake. "We should let our parents know we're safe."

Jolene laughed and shook her head. "Bob and me are a couple of old hippies. We're hopeless with modern stuff. I mean, look at this old van we've got."

"We're wasting time," said Bob, "let's get going."

"There's always time to help someone," said Jolene. She gave Maritska another hug and helped her into the camper-van.

The other car slowed down a bit as it passed the van.

---

2 **to blurt sth out** [ˈblɜːt ˌsʌmθɪŋ aʊt] mit etw. herausplatzen • 9 **to be concerned** [kənˈsɜːnd] besorgt sein • 15 **shiny** [ˈʃaɪni] glänzend • 18 **Doomadgee** [duːˈmædʒiː] *Stadt in Queensland* • 19 **according to** [əˈkɔːdɪŋ] nach

Jake noticed the two men in the car both had beards and wore black baseball caps pulled down low over their eyes. He thought it was odd that they didn't even look at them as they drove past. Jake was relieved Jolene and Bob were giving them a ride and not the weird looking guys in the black car. 5

• • •

Jake sat in the back of Bob and Jolene's van. As they drove off, he stared out of the window, hoping he'd catch a glimpse of Kyeema. He felt bad that they had parted without saying goodbye. 10

Jolene fished some Coca-Cola cans out of something she called an 'Esky'. It was a white polystyrene box filled with ice and water. The drinks were freezing cold. Pim, Maritska and Jake thankfully drank them in almost one gulp. Jolene switched the radio on. Pim and Maritska were 15 extremely happy to have contact with the familiar world again.

As some country and western music played in the background, Jolene told the kids why she and Bob were on the road. They were on their way to a music festival. 20 Jolene grabbed her guitar and began to play along to the radio. Then she started to sing along, too. Jake thought she was very good, but he wished everyone would be quiet. He wanted to keep the melody of Kyeema's song clear in his mind. 25

Maritska admired Jolene's jewellery.

"Here," Jolene took a turquoise necklace from round her neck. She put it on Maritska. "A gift for you, it'll bring you good luck. It did me." Jolene winked at Bob.

"Really?" Maritska proudly admired her new necklace 30 in the rear-view mirror. "It's so beautiful! I'll treasure it forever. Thank you." Maritska hugged Jolene.

---

1 **beard** [bɪəd] Bart • 9 **glimpse** [glɪmps] kurzer/flüchtiger Blick • 9 **to part** [pɑːt] auseinandergehen • 12 **Esky** *(Aust.)* ['eski] Kühlbox • 12 **polystyrene** [ˌpɒlɪ'staɪriːn] Styropor • 15 **gulp** [gʌlp] Schluck • 29 **to wink at sb** [wɪŋk] jmdm. zuzwinkern • 31 **rear-view mirror** [ˌrɪəvjuː 'mɪrə] Rückspiegel

Jake noticed that Bob didn't say much. He'd just let out a dry laugh every time Jolene said something funny. Jake also noticed Bob kept looking at the mirror, which seemed odd since the road was empty.

5 Pim started looking at things in the back of the van.

"Don't touch anything," Jake told him.

"It's OK. I'll be careful," said Pim, but he kept on wriggling around and playing with things.

After a while the music on the radio stopped and the news
10 came on. The main topic was a report on the sandstorms which had blown up in the past days. Several small planes had gone missing in the Northern Territory because of the bad weather. The newsreader continued with the next story, "Armed robbers who stole a million dollars from the
15 Darwin Cattle Auction are still on the run. Police warn the public to watch out for two bearded men. Anyone who sees them should call the police immediately. They are considered dangerous and should not be approached."

"I saw them," said Jake suddenly.

20 Bob switched off the radio. "Don't be silly," he laughed.

"I think they were the men in the black car which was behind you," Jake continued.

"What, the one that drove past when we picked you up?" asked Jolene.

25 "I saw them," insisted Jake. "Two men with beards wearing baseball caps."

The twinkling lights of a small town and the big yellow sign of a petrol station appeared in the distance.

"Look, look!" cried Pim. "We're nearly there!" Pim was
30 over-excited. He pulled out something that was stuffed down the back of the seat.

"After we've rung our parents, we must call the police," said Jake.

---

6 **to touch** [tʌtʃ] anfassen • 11 **several** ['sevrəl] mehrere • 14 **armed** [ɑːmd] bewaffnet • 18 **to approach sb** [əˈprəʊtʃ] sich jmdm. nähern • 27 **to twinkle** ['twɪŋkl] funkeln, blitzen • 28 **petrol station** ['petrl 'steɪʃn] Tankstelle • 30 **to stuff** [stʌf] stopfen

"Why would armed robbers take a quiet road like this?" said Jolene. "Forget about them. You kids need to get home as soon as you can after the day you've had."

"Police ask lots of questions. We've got no time for that. We've got to get to Doomadgee tonight," Bob said wearily. 5

"I still think we should tell someone," said Jake.

"I think you should forget it!" Bob said firmly.

"Bob!" said Jolene angrily. "Don't shout at him. He's just trying to do the right thing."

"There's the petrol station up ahead." Maritska laughed 10 and pointed at the lights. "We're nearly home!"

"This is funny," giggled Pim. "See what I'll look like as an old man."

The van swerved as Bob turned to see what Pim was talking about. 15

Pim was wearing a fake beard. "Here, Jake, I've got another one. Put it on. Let's see what you'll look like when you grow up!" Pim held out another fake beard for him.

A terrible silence filled the van.

5 **tonight** [tə'naɪt] heute Abend/Nacht • 14 **to swerve** [swɜ:v] ausscheren

Jake looked up. Jolene had turned round in her seat and stared at Pim. Her blue eyes weren't kind anymore; they were as cold as ice. "Bob," she said softly, "we've got a big problem."

5   Bob looked over his shoulder. "I should have never listened to you," he said to Jolene. "I should have run them over."

"If that black car hadn't come up behind us, it would have been an option," Jolene replied.

10   "There's the petrol station ahead," cried Pim.

Maritska jumped up in her seat as Bob made a U-turn.

"Why are we turning back?" she asked. "We're almost there."

"This would be all over if your nosy brother hadn't gone 15 snooping back there," said Jolene.

"Pim, I told you not to touch anything!" said Jake. Maritska's heart sank. "We won't say anything. I promise we won't," she said to Jolene.

"Sorry, love," Jolene said and patted Maritska's hand. 20 "We can't risk you telling the police."

"Pim!" Maritska looked at her brother angrily. "Why don't you ever do as you're told?"

"I'm sorry," said Pim. He realized they were heading back into the desert. He threw the fake beards down on 25 the floor.

Jake's heart pounded in his ears. He wished he had trusted Kyeema's instinct. They shouldn't have got in this van.

Jake had no idea where the couple were taking them. All 30 he knew was it would be somewhere bad.

---

12 **U-turn** ['juːtɜːn] 180°-Wende ● 15 **nosy** ['nəʊzi] neugierig ● 16 **to snoop** [snuːp] herumschnüffeln ● 20 **to pat** [pæt] tätscheln ● 27 **to pound** [paʊnd] pochen

Chapter 8   The mine shaft

Jolene forced Maritska into the back of the van with Jake and Pim. The three of them lost track of how long they had driven back along the road. The sun had nearly set and dark, purple clouds formed in the sky. A strong wind blew clouds of red sand from the roadside into the air. The van's 5
headlights made two orange shafts of light in the dust in front of them.

Without any warning Bob suddenly spun the steering wheel. The van left the road. They all had to hold on tightly as it rattled over rough ground. 10

"Why are we going off the road?" asked Jake nervously.

Maritska and Jake looked at each other fearfully. They were glad Pim was sleeping and couldn't see how scared they were.

The van's headlights suddenly fell on some rough 15
buildings. A tall, old chimney and a lift shaft rose in the sky before them.

Bob stopped the van. "End of the line. Everybody out," he barked. Jolene grabbed a torch and jumped out at the passenger side. 20

Jake and Maritska heard Bob and Jolene muttering as they walked round the van. "Should we make a run for it?" asked Maritska.

Jake nodded. "Pim, wake up," he said softly and shook him. 25

Pim's eyes opened slowly and he blinked sleepily. "Where are we? Why have we stopped?

"I don't know, but we've got to get away." Jake could still hear Bob and Jolene arguing outside the back of the van. "This way." 30

---

shaft [ʃɑːft] Schacht; Lichtstrahl • **6 headlight** [ˈhɛdlaɪt] Scheinwerfer •
8 steering wheel [ˈstɪərɪŋ ˌwiːl] Lenkrad • **16 chimney** [ˈtʃɪmni] Schornstein •
19 torch [tɒːtʃ] Taschenlampe

As quietly as they could, Jake, Maritska and Pim crawled into the front of the van. Without making a sound, Jake opened the door a little bit. "Stay low," he said.

The three of them slid out of the van. Jake pushed Pim
5 and Maritska in front of him.

"Run," hissed Jake. "Let's hope they don't –"

Bang! A gunshot rang out.

"You didn't think you'd get away that easily, did ya?"

They turned to see Bob standing next to the van. He
10 held a rifle. It was pointed in their direction.

"Come back," shouted Bob.

Nervously, the kids returned to the van.

"This way," Bob used the rifle to point the direction he wanted them to go.

15 Jolene had appeared at Bob's side.

"Just do as he says," Jolene whispered to them as they walked past her. The torch light fell on her face. They could see that Jolene was scared now, too.

The wind howled as Bob forced them towards the
20 buildings at the base of the shaky, metal tower.

"What is this place?" shouted Jake. He had to raise his voice against the wind in order to be heard.

"An old tin mine!" Bob shouted back. "Hasn't been used in fifty years. Nobody comes near it," he laughed, "except
25 for kids who get lost in the outback looking for shelter. Old mines are dangerous places. They've got deep shafts. Fall down one of them and you'd never be seen again."

Jolene looked worried. "Bob, you said we'd just lock them in?"

30 Bob kicked the front door of the shack at the base of the lift shaft. It swung open with a creak. "Go in there," he said.

"But Bob, you can't be serious," whispered Jolene.

---

6 **to hiss** [hɪs] zischen • 10 **rifle** ['raɪfl] Gewehr • 24 **except for** [ɪk'sept fə] außer • 25 **shelter** ['ʃeltə] Unterstand, Schutz • 28 **to lock sb up** ['lɒk] jmdn. einsperren • 30 **shack** [ʃæk] Bretterbude, Hütte • 31 **creak** [kriːk] Knarren

Bob waved the rifle in Jolene's direction. "This way there'll be no risk of them identifying us." As they walked inside, Jolene shone the torch around the shack.

Jake saw it was full of old machinery and rusty tools. At the far end was a half opened metal gate. Behind this was complete darkness. Jake realized it was the entrance to the lift shaft.

"Go to the shaft," Bob pushed Jake with the rifle. "All of you."

Jake's stomach tightened with fear. His mind raced as they walked towards the shaft.

"I'm scared," said Pim.

Jake placed his arm gently on his shoulder, "It'll be all right."

"We must do something," murmured Maritska.

Jake heard Bob and Jolene arguing quietly. Jolene waved her hands about as she talked. Light from her torch cast long shadows across the floor.

Jake spotted marks in the sand. They were wavy lines like the ones they had seen by the trees, the ones Maritska thought were made by someone drawing in the sand. He didn't just see a few tracks in the sand, he saw lots. The whole floor was covered with them.

"We need to play for time," Jake whispered. He stopped walking.

"Nobody told you to stop. Keep going towards the shaft," yelled Bob.

"Killing us would be a big mistake." Jake turned and faced Bob.

"Really? Give me one good reason why!"

"Our parents are very rich." Jake thought it was all right to tell a lie at a time like this. "They'd pay a lot of money to get us back."

Jake saw Bob's mind filter this information.

4 **tool** [tu:l] Werkzeug • 10 **to tighten sth** ['taɪtn] etw. zusammenziehen •
15 **to murmur** ['mɜːmɜː] raunen • 27 **to yell** [jel] schreien

"The kid has got a point," Jolene muttered to Bob. The two of them discussed it quietly together, glancing at the kids every now and then.

Jake's eyes raced around the inside of the shack. The light
5 of Jolene's torch was enough for him to see something move behind Bob's shoulder. Their arrival in the abandoned shack had woken up its sleeping inhabitants. Two large snakes moved silently along the rafters. Jake looked around and saw more snakes. They were coming out of
10 the shadows, crawling out from under old tarpaulins and buckets.

"Are you crazy, Jake?" said Maritska quietly. "Our parents aren't rich. What'll happen when they can't pay that much?"

15 Jake didn't answer. He watched the snake slide down from the rafter above Bob's head. "Sshh," said Jake. "No more questions." Jake grabbed Pim's hand and kicked Maritska, "Up there." He flicked his eyes to the roof.

6 **abandoned** [əˈbændənd] verlassen, leer stehend • 7 **inhabitant** [ɪnˈhæbɪtənt] Bewohner • 8 **rafter** [ˈrɑːftə] Dachsparren • 10 **tarpaulin** [tɑːˈpɔːlɪn] Abdeckplane • 11 **bucket** [ˈbʌkɪt] Eimer

Maritska held back a gasp as she saw the snake about to drop on Bob.

"When I say run, run," whispered Jake.

Bob broke off his discussion with Jolene and turned his attention back to the kids. "You bought yourself some 5 time. How much do you think your parents would pay to get you back? One million? Two million? What the – ?!" Bob's demands stopped in their tracks as the snake dropped onto his shoulder and slithered round his neck.

Bang! 10

Bob accidentally fired the rifle as the snake crawled along his arm. Luckily the bullet missed them all. Bob yelled hysterically as he tried to shake the snake off his arm.

"Run!" Jake screamed at Maritska. Jake took Pim by the 15 hand. They raced around Bob.

"Oh my God, they're everywhere. This whole place is alive with them!" Jolene screamed as snakes slithered around her feet.

"Get it off me!" Bob begged Jolene. 20

Although she was terrified, Jolene managed to pull the snake off Bob. She threw it to the other side of the shack.

"The stupid thing bit me!" cried Bob. His eyes bulged at the sight of two red spots on his hand.

Jake, Maritska and Pim ran out of the shack as fast as 25 their legs would carry them. When they got outside, they were surrounded by the sandstorm.

"Which way now?" cried Maritska. She coughed and covered her mouth to stop sand blowing in it.

"That snake could be poisonous!" The kids heard Jolene 30 cry as she and Bob stumbled out of the mine.

"I can't let them get away," Bob shouted. "I don't want to go back to prison."

---

8 **demand** [dɪˈmɑːnd] Forderung ▪ 9 **to slither** [ˈslɪðə] gleiten ▪ 12 **bullet** [ˈbʊlɪt] Kugel ▪ 23 **to bulge** [bʌldʒ] hervortreten ▪ 30 **poisonous** [ˈpɔɪznəs] giftig

"If you don't get help for that bite, you could die!" Jolene's torch light shone through the dust.

"They can't have got far," Bob said. "Where have you gone?" he shouted into the night.

5   "Leave them," said Jolene. "We need to get you to a doctor."

Jake held his breath and prayed for help. "Kyeema, I wish you were here," he said to himself. "Give me a hint which way to go."

10   Then, and it was only for a moment, the wind dropped and the sky cleared. Although it was only a dot on the horizon, Jake recognized the large rock from Kyeema's song – the resting place of the lizard ancestor. Jake's mind snapped into gear. Going back along the road and turning
15   off to the mine, he realized they weren't that far from where Kyeema had first found them. If he could get them to the rock, he thought they might be able to find their way.

"I see them," yelled Bob. Bang! A shot rang out and a bullet whistled past their ears.

20   "Follow me," Jake ordered. He ran in the direction of the rock. With no hesitation this time, Maritska and Pim raced after him. The wind suddenly picked up. Dust was in the air and hid them from Bob and Jolene.

"You stupid kids!" they heard Bob shout after them.
25   "You're alone in the outback. You won't last the night!" Bob fired one final shot in their direction.

Jake worried that if the dust storm went on much longer, they truly would be lost. As they raced into the night, Jake hoped he had made the right decision and was leading his
30   brother and sister to safety and not into more danger.

---

7 to pray [preɪ] beten • **14 to snap into gear** [snæp ˌɪntə ˈɡɪə] in Gang kommen •
21 hesitation [ˌhezɪˈteɪʃn] Zögern • **28 truly** [ˈtruːli] wahrhaftig

Chapter 9   The longest night

"Stop, stop!" Maritska gasped. She bent down and tried to catch her breath.

The wind had died down and several stars twinkled in the sky.

"Are they still after us?" asked Pim. 5

Jake listened. Apart from the distant cry of the dingoes the night was silent. "The snake bite scared Bob. I bet he's looking for a doctor right now."

Pim and Jake noticed that Maritska was having difficulty breathing. 10

"What's wrong?" asked Jake.

"I don't know." Her voice was faint, no more than a croak. "While we were running in the sandstorm, I must have breathed in some sand."

"Take a moment. You'll be fine," said Jake reassuringly. 15

Maritska rubbed her throat. Her hand fell on the turquoise necklace that Jolene had given her. She ripped it off and flung it as far as she could. "Would they have really pushed us down that mine shaft?"

"If money is the most important thing in your life, then 20 you do crazy things." Jake's fear was that after Bob had received treatment for the snake bite he'd return and look for them. They had to get back to the road before Bob had time to get better. "Are you OK to go on?"

Maritska covered her mouth and she coughed. She tried 25 hard to catch her breath. "I don't feel well. I can't walk anymore."

"Kyeema! Kyeema!" Pim shouted. "Please come. We need your help again!"

They all looked up in the hope they'd see her running 30 towards them. But nobody came.

---

12 **faint** [feɪnt] matt • 15 **to reassure** [ˌriːəˈʃʊə] beruhigen • 16 **throat** [θrəʊt] Hals • 18 **to fling sth** [flɪŋ] etw. schleudern, werfen

"There are some bushes near the rock," Jake said and pointed to an area of scrub which was silhouetted by the moon. "You can rest there a while."

Pim and Jake helped Maritska. Every step made her
5 gasp for breath. Before they laid her under a small tree, Jake checked for snake marks on the ground. There were none, so there was one danger less to face.

"I really think I'm sick" croaked Maritska.

"You'll be fine," Jake said, but he imagined that terrible
10 things could happen. Maritska had been very ill a few years ago. A bad cold had turned into pneumonia and she had had to go to hospital. She was so sick that their parents had flown home from the US to be with her. Jake overheard them talking one night. They were worried her
15 illness might be fatal. However, after a few days when her life hung in the balance, she recovered. But the doctors warned that it might have damaged her lungs. Jake guessed a combination of exhaustion and inhaling the dust had placed too much of a strain on her body.
20 "I see something!" Pim shouted.

Two small points of light flickered in the night.

"Is it her?" asked Maritska hopefully. "Has Kyeema come to help us?"

The lights came closer and they realized it was the moon
25 reflecting off an animal's eyes.

"Oh no," Maritska trembled. "It's a wild dog. It's going to attack us!" Her body was shaken by a bad coughing fit.

The dingo broke into a run and jumped towards them.

Jake stood still. For some reason he wasn't scared. He
30 remembered Kyeema had told him that old people in her village believed the dingoes were part of their tribe.

The dog stopped at Jake's feet. Its amber eyes looked up into his for a moment. The dog threw its head back and howled. It paused and then howled again. This time the

---

2 **scrub** [skrʌb] Gestrüpp • 11 **pneumonia** [njuːˈməʊniə] Lungenentzündung •
15 **fatal** [ˈfeɪtl] tödlich • 16 **to recover** [rɪˈkʌvə] gesund werden • 18 **exhaustion**
[ɪgˈzɔːstʃn] Erschöpfung • 19 **strain** [streɪn] Belastung

bark was a deeper tone. The sound resonated in Jake's mind.

"Pim, stay here and look after her." Jake knelt down and placed his hand on Maritska's. "I'll get help."

Pim watched Maritska's eyes flicker as she strained for 5
breath. "But how, Jake? We don't know where we are!"

Jake forced himself not to panic. The dingo's bark echoed in his head. The desert dog trotted away. Jake didn't move. He was humming a tune. It was familiar.

The moonlight shone on the big rock of the lizard 10
ancestor which loomed over them. Jake remembered Kyeema's song. He opened his mouth and began to sing. He wasn't the greatest singer, but the tune easily rang out in the night.

Pim looked up at Jake as if he was mad, "How can you 15
sing at a time like this?"

"It's the songline! I have to sing it to show me the way." Jake didn't know the words to Kyeema's song, but he could remember the story. The tune would tell him whether the terrain was smooth or rocky and the story would show the 20
landmarks he needed to know he was on the right path. "If I remember it right and run all the way I should find the road again by sunrise."

They stared at their sister trying hard to catch her breath. 25

"If I had listened to you and done as I was told none of this would have happened," said Pim sadly.

"We can't think about that now," Jake ruffled Pim's curly red hair. "Now is the time for us to stop making mistakes and do things right." 30

Jake looked up and saw the dingo. It stood in the distance and stared back at him. Jake took a deep breath. He cleared his mind and thought of the story Kyeema told

---

1 **to resonate** [ˈrezneɪt] (wider)hallen • 3 **to kneel** [niːl] knien • 9 **to hum** [hʌm] summen • 9 **tune** [tjuːn] Melodie • 11 **to loom** [luːm] sich drohend abzeichnen

him. "There's one thing you need to do for me," Jake said to Pim who looked very scared.

"What's that?" asked Pim.

"Stay safe until morning." Jake took one last look at
5 Maritska and Pim and waved goodbye.

Jake ran to where the dingo waited for him. As soon he caught up with it, the dingo began to run too. Together they raced into the night.

• • •

10 Jake was thankful that the night was cool. He ran like the wind. He could never have kept up this pace in the heat of the day. He didn't know where his energy came from, but somehow his feet kept moving. And he was not alone, the whole time the dingo kept up with him.

15 At one point Jake was so thirsty he thought he was going to faint. As if it could sense his need, the dingo ran off over a dune and disappeared. Jake went to see where it had gone. He found the animal drinking from a water hole. Jake followed and drank at its side.

20 When he got hungry and his energy was low, Jake found some quandong and he knew they were good to eat. He hoped he reached help before morning and didn't have to eat witchetty grubs and ants. But if he did have to, he knew where he was likely to find them. He was not afraid.

25 Although it was extremely important that he reached civilisation to get help for his sister, Jake was amazed by the moonlit beauty of the outback. The way his feet moved across the earth in time to the rhythm of the music in his head gave him a sense of connection to the land.

30 Each time he began to doubt and thought he might be going the wrong way, he'd spot a landmark which reminded him that he was on the right path. He saw the group of hills where the song said the lizard had laid its eggs. The deep grooves which were made when the babies

11 **pace** [peɪs] tempo • 16 **to faint** [feɪnt] ohnmächtig werden •
17 **dune** [djuːn] Düne

crawled away. The valley which was flooded by the lizard's tears when it cried about the loss of its children.

The sky was changing. Black was becoming blue. The rising sun threw shades of pink and orange on the clouds.

But then Jake came to a sudden halt. He was confused. 5 Two hills of similar height lay in the distance. The one to the left was rocky and uneven, while the one to the right was smooth. He sang the song out loud. "That's it!" he said happily. The song's notes were short and high and low. The song was telling him to go to the rocky hill. He began 10 to run as fast as he could to the hill on the left.

"Grrrr …" the dingo let out a low growl, raced after Jake and jumped at him.

Jake felt the dingo's jaws clamp around his arm. "Let go!" he cried out in surprise. 15

Jake fell to the ground and tried to drag his arm out of the animal's mouth. But its bite was strong. "Get off! I must get help! If I take too long my sister could die." Jake thought he was crazy, talking to a wild dog. But he felt the animal had been helping him. He couldn't understand why it 20 would attack him now. He also couldn't understand why he didn't feel its teeth in his arm.

Then, suddenly, the dingo opened its mouth and let go.

Jake quickly crawled away and got back on his feet. He began to run to the hill on the left. He had only gone a few 25 steps before the dingo jumped on him again. This time it didn't try and bite. Jake stopped.

The dingo gazed up at him. Their eyes met.

Jake didn't know if he was imagining it, but it was as if he heard it say, "Follow me …" 30

Jake was sure he should go to the hill on the left. But he remembered the times when he should have listened to someone else. The time Pim said they were going the wrong way at the airport, and when Kyeema told him not

---

5 **confused** [kən'fjuːzd] verwirrt • 6 **similar** ['sɪmɪlə] ähnlich • 6 **height** [haɪt] Höhe • 12 **growl** [graʊl] Knurren • 14 **jaw** [dʒɔː] Maul, Kiefer • 14 **to clamp sth** [klæmp] etw. festhalten

to get in Bob and Jolene's van. Perhaps it was a crazy thing to do, but this time Jake felt he should listen to what this creature was telling him.

"You want me to go this way? OK. I'll follow you. Will that make you happy?" Jake asked the dingo. It immediately raced off towards the smooth hill on the right. After only a moment's pause, Jake followed.

As he ran, Jake was afraid he had made a big mistake. But as he got closer he saw the hill to his right wasn't smooth. When he saw it from a different perspective he could tell it was rocky. Jake felt like his lungs were going to burst. The hill was close. He saw the jagged stones on its side. Jake's heart jumped. Large piles of rocks lay ahead. He could breathe as he climbed up the rocks. Was the road on the other side? The dingo walked noisily on the rocks as it followed him.

Jake reached the top of the hill.

The whole landscape spread out before him. A breathtaking sunrise brought the Australian outback to

11 **to burst** [bɜːst] platzen • 12 **jagged** [ˈdʒægɪd] zerklüftet

life. Kangaroos jumped gently across the undulating plain. Colourful budgerigars flew across the sky. But Jake was extremely happy to see something more beautiful than nature's wonders. There was the road! Even better, there were two lorries and a couple of cars heading his way. 5

"We made it!" Jake said to the dingo by his side.

The dingo stood on the top of the rock pile and watched Jake climb down to the road.

Jake stopped the first lorry. It slowed down as soon as the driver saw him. The driver had an ultra-modern 10 communication rig. He immediately asked the emergency services to call an air ambulance for Maritska.

The other lorry and the cars pulled to a halt. After what seemed like an eternity of being alone in the outback, Jake found himself surrounded by people. Jake noticed that two 15 days in the sun had turned his skin dark brown. Together with his thick, black hair this made the people on the road think he was an Aborigine when they first saw him. Jake told them his whole story. The drivers were surprised by his skill and bravery at surviving in the bush. They patted 20 him on the back and said things like, 'Bonza', 'Good on yer mate' and 'Well done, cobber.'

Jake didn't understand all their Aussie slang, but their voices were full of praise. However, Jake didn't allow himself any time for pride. He could think about being 25 proud of himself when he knew his brother and sister had been rescued and Maritska was all right.

There was so much going on, so many questions and so much to think about, Jake forgot to check if the dingo was still at the top of the hill. 30

If he had looked up, he would have seen that it was waiting. It stayed where it was and watched over him until he got in the lorry. It stayed and watched until the cars and

---

1 **undulating** [ˈʌndjəleɪtɪŋ] sanft geschwungen • 1 **plain** [pleɪn] Ebene •
2 **budgerigar** [ˈbʌdʒɪrɪɡɑː] Wellensittich • 11 **rig** [rɪɡ] Vorrichtung, Anlage •
21 **bonza** *(coll., Aust.)* [ˈbɒnzɑː] cool, genial • 21 **Good on yer!** *(coll., Aust.)*
[ɡʊd ɒn jeə] Gut gemacht! • 22 **cobber** [ˈkɒbə] Kumpel • 24 **praise** [preɪz] Lob

lorries drove away and the road was empty once more. It waited until Jake's lorry was a tiny dot on the horizon. Only then did it pick its way down the rocks. Within moments, its sand coloured fur and amber eyes blended with the
5   landscape and the dingo disappeared from view.

Chapter 10   Australians

Jake's heart pounded heavily all the way to the petrol station. The lorry driver used his radio system to put him on to the emergency service operator. Jake described, as best he could, the location where he had left Maritska and
10 Pim. Luckily the landmarks he described made sense to the operator.

By the time they pulled into the gas station, Jake heard the sound of helicopter blades overhead. Two choppers flew low and headed towards the outback.
15 There was a small snack bar in the petrol station. The waitress immediately brought Jake something to eat and drink.

"Have you got a phone?" he asked her.

It wasn't until somebody placed a mobile in his hand
20 that he realized he had no idea of his parents' number. The information he needed to contact everybody was on his mobile phone. He didn't have anything at all written on a piece of paper. Normally, this was fine. But now his phone was lost, probably broken, in the middle of the outback.
25 It made Jake realize how dependent the modern world had become on electronic equipment and computers to communicate and survive.

---

7 radio system [ˈreɪdiəʊ ˌsɪstəm] Funksystem • **8 emergency service operator** [ɪˈmɜːdʒnsi sɜːvɪs ˌɒpreɪtə] Notdienstmitarbeiter • **13 helicopter blade** [ˈhelɪkɒptə ˌbleɪd] Hubschrauberrotor • **13 chopper** [ˈtʃɒpə] Hubschrauber • **14 to head towards sth** [hed təˈwɔːdz] auf etw. zusteuern

Jake heard the 'whoop, whoop' of a siren from the forecourt. A police car pulled up. Two officers jumped out and hurried in. People pointed them in Jake's direction.

"OK, son," one of the officers said. "We've spoken to your parents. They're on their way." 5

Jake was relieved that his parents knew where they were and that he'd see them soon. The police told him that several search parties had been out looking for them. As it turned out, Ray had moved so far from his flight plan to avoid the sandstorm that they had been searching in the 10 wrong area.

After Jake described the accident, the police told him that they had only survived because of Ray's skill as a pilot. Two other planes had been caught in the sudden sandstorm, too. Both of them had lost control and crashed. 15 There were no survivors in either accident.

A message came through on one of the policeman's walkie-talkies. The officer smiled and shook Jake's hand. "No worries," he said. "They've found them."

"Are they all right?" Jake asked. "Is Maritska OK?" 20

After a short interchange the policeman nodded. "They're taking her to Darwin. She'll have to stay in hospital. They got to her just in time. If you had taken a couple of hours more, they don't think she'd have made it." 25

At last Jake could relax.

The policemen were about to turn away when Jake jumped up. "There's something else I need to tell you! It's about the people who robbed the cattle auction."

Everyone in the petrol station fell silent. They turned to 30 Jake and stared at him.

"I know who they are."

• • •

2 forecourt ['fɔːkɔːt] Vorhof • 10 to avoid [ə'vɔɪd] ausweichen, vermeiden • 16 no ... either [nəʊ] ... ['aɪðə] keine/-r/-s (der beiden) • 21 interchange ['ɪntətʃeɪndʒ] Austausch

The next few days were a blur to Jake. The police quickly brought him back to Darwin where he met Maritska and Pim again at the hospital. Their parents were at her bedside.

5   After lots of hugs and some tears from their mother, they told the story of their ordeal in the desert.

"I'm so sorry," said their dad. "This wasn't the way we wanted you to arrive here."

"I know you didn't want to come to Australia," their 10 mother patted Maritska's hand. She looked at all the kids, "I guess you'll want to go back to Holland as soon as you can."

Pim's eyes widened. "Oh, no! Back home was sooo boring! This is the most exciting thing that has ever 15 happened to me."

"Excuse me," Maritska corrected him. "We had a plane crash, walked a whole day across the desert, had to escape from armed robbers and I'm in hospital!"

"I thought it was fun," muttered Pim.

20   "There's something we need to talk about." Their parents stood up and faced them. "You didn't know Ray for very long, but he was a wonderful man. He didn't have any kids of his own. He was looking forward to all of you coming to live at the station. We told him so much about 25 you he felt like you were already part of the family. He left us some papers in the event that anything should happen to him. We opened them on the way here after we heard he had died."

Their father handed Jake a letter. It had 'Last Will and 30 Testament of Raymond Cooper Argyle' written on the top.

Jake scanned the document quickly.

"How you kids feel about this country could influence the rest of our lives," said their dad.

---

1 blur [blɜ:] Unschärfe, undeutliches Bild • **6 ordeal** [ɔ:ˈdi:l] Tortur, Leidensweg • **17 to escape** [ɪˈskeɪp] flüchten, fliehen

"What is it?" asked Pim. Maritska groaned as he climbed across her bed to look at the letter.

"He left the cattle station to us?" Jake couldn't quite believe what he was reading.

"He wanted a family to own it, a family who would make 5 it their home. We brought you here to live with us for the rest of our work contract. We didn't want our family to be apart any longer. It would have been for a couple of years," their mother said.

"But now you're talking about us living here for the rest 10 of our lives," said Jake.

Their mum and dad nodded gravely.

"It's your decision, kids. After we thought we had lost you, we felt so bad. We'd put our work ahead of you too many times. Whether we stay here, or go back to Holland, 15 will be up to you to decide."

Maritska, Pim and Jake looked at each other. After all the years of arguments and annoyance, the trauma of the past couple of days had somehow brought them closer together. 20

"Take some time to see how you like it here," their mother said. "It'll be up to you which place you want to call home."

• • •

They all stayed in Darwin for a few days until Maritska was discharged from hospital. 25

It felt strange going back to the airfield for their flight to Argyle Downs. Their parents had hired a pilot with a larger plane, so they could all travel together. This time their whole journey was clear and smooth.

They landed on a small airstrip. Several large houses 30 with verandas were dotted around. Instead of the red desert, they were surrounded by green fields and trees.

---

1 **to groan** [grəʊn] stöhnen • 8 **to be apart** [bɪ əˈpɑːt] getrennt sein • 26 **to discharge sb** [dɪsˈtʃɑːdʒ] *hier:* jmdn. entlassen • 31 **airstrip** [ˈeəstrɪp] Landebahn

They could hear the moos of brown and white cows grazing on the hills.

After they had had a quick look around, the kids ran into the house. They had been allowed to choose their 5 own rooms. The station house was huge and so were the rooms.

Maritska chose a large room at the back. It had lots of shade and a small balcony. Pim picked one with an unusual round window which had a writing desk in front 10 of it. Jake's room was at the front of the house. It had a view of the sunset and distant red hills. Every one of the kids felt happy with their choice.

After they had settled in, Jake often thought of Kyeema. He was sorry he hadn't had the chance to thank her for 15 coming to their rescue that night after the crash.

Jake became friendly with some of the Aboriginal men who worked on the station. One of them, whose name was Jimmy, knew the Yolngu settlement in Arnhem Land where Kyeema said she lived. He offered to take Jake there. Jake wondered if they'd have to walk. Jimmy replied with an 20 Aussie, "No worries". He had a jeep and they could drive.

• • •

The Yolngu settlement was a collection of low shacks. Jake didn't know where to begin to look for Kyeema. Jimmy saw a couple of old Aboriginal men sitting in the 25 sun. One of them had white lines painted on his face, the other wore a checked shirt and had straggly grey hair. "Let's ask those old blokes," he said.

The men didn't speak English well, but luckily Jimmy spoke a couple of Aboriginal dialects. Jake heard Jimmy 30 say some things he didn't understand, but when he said 'Kyeema' the men leant forward. Jimmy said 'Kyeema' again. This time the men looked worried. They had a short conversation and exchanged some words with Jimmy.

---

1 moo [mu:] Muhen • 2 to graze [greɪz] grasen • 8 balcony ['bælkəni] Balkon •
13 to settle in ['setl] sich einleben • 18 Arnhem Land ['ɑ:nəm lænd] *Region im Northern Territory* • 26 straggly ['strægli] zottelig • 27 bloke [bləʊk] Kerl

"Do they know where she lives?" asked Jake.

"They think you've had too much sun," Jimmy told him as they walked away. They got back in the jeep.

"She's not here then?" Jake was disappointed.

As they drove back to Argyle Downs, Jimmy explained 5 why the men had acted oddly. They did know of a girl called Kyeema. She wanted to do something important with her life. She wanted to change the world. She was frustrated that the boys got to have all the adventures while the girls stayed at home. So one day she went on a walkabout. 10

"I know," said Jake. "That's where I met her."

"No way, mate," said Jimmy. "A sandstorm blew up a few days after she had left. When it cleared they think she was in a place she didn't recognize because she hadn't been taught all the words of the songs. She never came back." 15

Jake was confused. "What do they mean never? She only went on a walkabout a few days ago."

"No mate," replied Jimmy, "this was sixty years ago. The old men say there's a dingo people see from time to time. They think it's Kyeema. It reminds the old people she lost 20 her way because they wouldn't teach her all of the sacred knowledge because she was a girl. They feel guilty when someone sees the dingo. It reminds people they have to change."

Jake was lost in thought as Jimmy started the jeep and 25 they drove back to Argyle Downs.

• • •

Jake sat on the gate of one of the cattle pens. Pim was reading out loud to him. They had electricity on the ranch, but it would often fail. The Internet signal was weak and Pim got bored with losing the connection all the time. Pim 30 had started writing, with a pen and on paper! Every night he'd sit at his desk in front of the round window and write stories. Pim had a wild imagination. His stories were crazy, but they were funny. It had become a new routine that

4 **disappointed** [ˌdɪsəˈpɔɪntɪd] enttäuscht • 22 **guilty** [ˈgɪlti] schuldig •
27 **pen** [pen] *hier:* Umzäunung, Pferch • 29 **to fail** [feɪl] *hier:* ausfallen

61

every evening, before dinner, they would sit in the yard and Pim would read out what he had written the day before.

The sound of hooves interrupted them. Maritska galloped up on a tall horse. She took off her wide-brimmed
5 hat. Her blonde hair dropped down.

Jake thought it was funny that a girl who had once worried herself silly about clothes now wore jeans and boots most of the time. She had had a few riding lessons back in Holland. At first she was nervous about getting in
10 the saddle, but once she got back on a horse, she found she loved it. She'd go for a ride around the station every evening, checking the fences and helping the workers at the cattle station.

"Good news," cried Maritska as she jumped off her
15 horse and tied it to the fence. "The cops caught Bob and Jolene!"

"Where did they find them?" asked Pim.

---

3 **hoof, hooves** *(pl.)* [hu:f], [hu:vz] der Huf/die Hufe • 10 **saddle** ['sædl] Sattel •
12 **fence** [fens] Zaun

"Getting on a flight out of Brisbane. They'd have probably escaped if we hadn't given the police their description."

"Good," cried Jake. "Nice work, team!" The three of them slapped their hands together in a high-five.

Maritska climbed up on the fence and sat next to Jake. 5 "So have you decided?" She looked at Pim and Jake.

"I have," said Pim.

"Me too," said Jake.

"So we know which country we want to call home?" They nodded to each other. 10

"We're going to be Australians!" shouted Pim. He jumped up on the fence next to Jake.

Without doubting that they had made the right choice, the three of them laughed and joked as the last rays of golden sun brought the day to an end. 15

"Kids! Dinner is on the table!" Their mother's voice echoed from the house.

Maritska jumped down and led her horse to the stable. Pim gathered his papers and ran towards the house. One thing he was never late for was meals. 20

Jake watched the sunset a moment longer. He had never told the others what the old men had said about Kyeema. He was worried his family would think he was crazy if he thought her spirit was the dingo which ran with him during that long night. 25

Jake thought Australia's endless outback could be deadly, but it also held great wonders and beauty. Kyeema was born of this land. She too could be harsh and brutal, but also kind and funny. Maybe that was Australia's gift to him. It could be a dangerous place, but if you learned to 30 respect and trust it, it could be the most incredible place to live. Kyeema would always mean Australia to him, and he knew in his heart that would mean home.

---

4 **high-five** [haɪˈfaɪv] Abklatschen • 13 **to doubt** [daʊt] zweifeln • 14 **ray** [reɪ] Strahl • 18 **stable** [ˈsteɪbl] Stall • 19 **to gather** [ˈɡæðə] (ein)sammeln • 28 **harsh** [hɑːʃ] rau, barsch • 31 **incredible** [ɪnˈkredɪbl] wunderbar, unglaublich

Jake jumped off the fence and knelt down. He dug his fingers deep into the red soil. Something in him echoed with the vibration of the earth. After a moment he dusted the dirt from his hand, stood up and slowly walked back to
5 the house. The sounds of his family sitting down to dinner echoed from inside. "Don't eat yet, Pim. Wait for your brother," he heard his dad say.

"Hurry up, Jake!" Pim yelled out the door. "I'm so hungry!" Jake broke into a trot. There was no mention
10 between them of adoption or being half-brothers and sister anymore. Jake finally felt he belonged to this family, and to this country.

As he ran to the house, Jake decided that tonight was the night he'd tell the whole family what the old men had said
15 about Kyeema. He'd tell them how he truly believed she was the dingo. If that dingo hadn't stopped him, he would have run to the wrong hill. If he had made that mistake it would have taken him hours to get back to the road. The doctors said that delay would have cost Maritska's life.
20 And Jake wouldn't worry if they laughed at him! Maybe they wouldn't believe it; perhaps they'd think it was all just a crazy story. But then Kyeema had said she wanted to change the world and be a person in a story.

Jake took a second to look at the evening sky before
25 he went into the house. A bright star shone in the dusk. Jake suddenly realized that Kyeema had done what she had set out to do. She had changed their lives. He owed it to Kyeema to tell her story to anyone who would listen. He'd make sure the girl who went on a walkabout all those
30 years ago would not be forgotten.

Kyeema's wish really had come true.

---

2 **soil** [sɔɪl] Erde • 4 **dirt** [dɜːt] Dreck, Schmutz • 11 **to belong to sb** [bɪˈlɒŋ] zu jmdm. gehören • 25 **dusk** [dʌsk] Dämmerung

While you read

1 A word search

Look at the German words below. They are all about the topic 'IT' and some are in chapter 1 and 2 of this reader. Find their English translations in this table. Some are two or three words written together.

A	J	I	T	M	K	T	E	R	A	B	Y	T	E
I	R	Z	T	O	S	T	O	R	E	E	V	C	Q
C	O	M	P	U	T	E	R	G	A	M	E	H	D
H	N	S	F	S	D	C	L	P	E	R	O	B	T
T	J	R	M	E	U	H	X	G	O	W	U	P	O
O	D	O	X	B	Y	N	E	T	W	O	R	K	S
L	E	A	T	G	C	O	M	N	Q	B	Y	T	E
O	S	M	O	B	I	L	E	P	H	O	N	E	T
G	K	I	T	O	D	O	W	N	L	O	A	D	U
O	T	N	Y	S	I	G	N	A	L	S	F	V	P
N	O	G	P	K	E	Y	B	O	A	R	D	T	A
K	P	L	E	T	O	S	W	I	T	C	H	O	N

Computerspiel, Netzwerk, Terabyte, Byte, Signal, Mobiltelefon, Technologie, Roaming, Tastatur, Maus, Arbeitsplatz, einschalten, einloggen, einstellen, abspeichern, herunterladen, tippen

2 A word web

Make a word web about one of the following topics: plane, airport or entertainment. Use words from chapters 1 and 2.

3 A crossword puzzle

Complete the crossword puzzle.

ACROSS:
1. The kids don't live with their ...
2. They are from ...
3. They are on their way to ...
4. Their parents work as ...
5. Pim is glad that there is ... on the farm.

DOWN:
In the beginning of the story, the kids are on a ...

4 The main characters

1. *Make a grid like this. Then describe Jake, Maritska and Pim. The words below will help you.*

Jake	Mariska	Pim
...		

techno geek • fifteen • careless • cheeky • trustworthy • hair the colour of carrots • princess • cosmetics • lonely • bored • thoughtful • excited • tired • responsible • pretty • no sense of direction • long blonde hair • cough • twelve • melancholic • full of energy • curly black hair

2. *Add more information about each of the characters as you continue to read. How have the kids changed in the end?*

5 True or false

When a plane crashes, passengers are told to get into the 'brace position'. Decide if the following statements are true or false.

1. In the brace position you push back into your seat, tighten your seat-belt, and lean forward so that your head touches the seat in front of you. Your feet are flat on the floor.
2. In the brace position you put your head on your knees, place your hands one on top of the other and on top of your head. Your fingers should not be interlocked. Your forearms are held against each side of your face.
3. The brace position is recommended so that people's teeth will stay intact during a crash. This helps to later identify people who have not survived.
4. It has not been proven that the brace position helps to prevent injuries.
5. In an accident in the past, passengers were asleep on a plane that was about to crash into some trees. One passenger woke up and adopted the brace position. He was the only survivor.
6. In over 70% of all airline accidents it is possible to survive.

6 Good news and bad news

Complete the table with information from chapter 3.

good news	bad news
…	

7 A mysterious girl

After reading chapter 4, collect information about the girl who saves the kids' lives by catching the snake. Who do you think she is?

8 Aboriginal culture

1. *What do we learn about the culture, traditions, problems and conflicts of the Aborigines in chapters 5 and 6?*

2. *List the survival techniques given in the text.*

9 The old world and the new world

"I love modern things, too, but I value the knowledge you've taught me. Surely there's a way the old world and the new can live side by side?"

1. *What do you think about this statement? Can the old world and the new world live side by side? Do you know any examples where this is the case?*

2. *Are modern ways always better than the old ways? Think of mobile phones, computers, social networks, chat rooms, cars, industrial biology, fast food, etc.*

3. *What old or old-fashioned things do you, your parents, or your grandparents still use today?*

4. *Discuss the pros and cons, the advantages and disadvantages or the risks and dangers of modern and old ways.*

10 Telling lies

Jake tells a lie in order to save their lives.

Is it all right to tell a lie in a situation like this? Are there any situations in which telling a lie is all right?
Have you ever been in a situation in which you thought it was right to tell a lie? Why did you think it was right?

11 The outback

Describe what the outback looks like.

12 Jake and the lorry drivers

Work in groups of four. One of you is Jake and the others are the lorry drivers. Create a dialogue.
What are the lorry drivers' questions and Jake's answers? Act out the scene.

Solutions

Before you read
Multiple choice

1. a;   2. c;   3. b;   4. b;   5. a

While you read

1   A word search

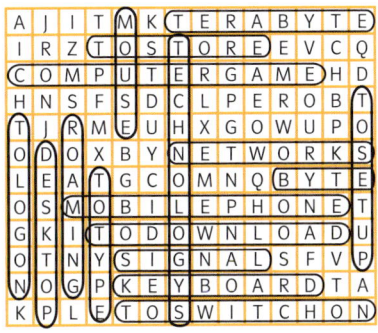

2   A word web

plane: seat, entertainment system, armrest, row, table, tail, breakfast tray, (plane) window, flight, double-deck jet, overhead locker, passenger, video screen, 'fasten seat belts' sign, turbulence, flight attendant, intercom, (plane) engine, to roar, captain, (cabin) crew, announcement, flight attendant, steward

airport: connecting flight, gangway, duty free shop, passport, baggage claim, car hire desk, customs, immigration department's booth, to scan, to stamp, trolley, security, customs barrier, traveller, terminal, ATM, Foreign Exchange desk, taxi sign, car park

entertainment: movie, channel, remote control, game, computer, entertainment system, video screen, to switch on

3   A crossword puzzle

Across: 1. parents, 2. Holland, 3. Australia, 4. scientists, 5. electricity; **Down:** plane

4   The main characters

1. **Jake:** trustworthy, lonely, thoughtful, responsible, no sense of direction, melancholic, curly black hair

Maritska: fifteen, princess, cosmetics, bored, tired, pretty, long blonde hair, cough

Pim: techno geek, careless, cheeky, hair the colour of carrots, excited, twelve, full of energy

2. **Jake:** protective, courageous, fascinated by Kyeema, smart, eager to learn, more self-confident, closer to nature, feels like he belongs to the family

Maritska: scared, disgusted by eating strange things, weak, sick, becoming more practical, rides a horse, wears jeans and boots, checks fences, helps workers

Pim: wants to be friends with Kyeema, curious, learns to listen to others, writes stories, less dependent on technology

5   True or false

1. True;   2. True;   3. False;   4. False;   5. True;   6. True

6   Good news and bad news

Good news: Ray manages to land on a sandbank. Jake, Maritska and Pim are alive and unhurt. They manage to exit the plane before it explodes. The trees and bushes provide shade. They find Maritska's bag with hats in it. Pim has got his mobile phone. **Bad news:** Ray has died from a heart attack. Jake cannot call for help because the headset doesn't work anymore. The plane explodes. The battery of Pim's mobile phone is dead. It's hot and very sunny. There's no water. They are alone in the middle of the outback.

7   A mysterious girl

She has thick wavy black hair and is dressed in a bikini made of brown animal skins. Her teeth are white and her eyes sparkling. On her back she carries a pack of white sticks. With one of them she kills a snake and saves the kids' lives. She might be an Aboriginal girl.

8   Aboriginal culture

1. In the Yolgnu tribe there is a conflict between the old ways and the modern world. The government thinks that Aboriginal kids are missing out on education and job opportunities, so some of them are sent to live with white families. The problem is that the old members of the tribe don't like change. The tribe has got a lot of history, but some of its older members only live in the past and are not open to modern ways. Because of that, as she is a girl, Kyeema is not supposed to go on walkabouts and she is not taught all the words of her tribe's songs. These songs tell stories from the Dreamtime, a period before living memory when spirits came out of the earth and down from the sky to create the land and all living things. The words of these songs are secret and must not be taught to anybody who is not part of the tribe. There is a connection between the songs and the landscape. When the notes are long and in the same tone the landscape is flat and empty, when they are faster and higher, the land is high and uneven. Aborigines believe that certain animals are your totem. They watch over you and are sacred. If a dingo is your totem, you are not allowed to kill it.

2. Eat snake meat. Collect sticks and pile them up to make a fire. Follow animal tracks to find food and water. Red fruits are usually good to eat, yellow ones are not. If something does not look good to eat, it probably isn't. Don't carry too many things with you.

9 The old world and the new world
Individual answers

10 Telling lies
Individual answers

11 The outback
The outback is a desert landscape. There are some hills, rocks and bushes. Sometimes the landscape is smooth, sometimes it is rocky and uneven. You can see breathtaking sunrises.

12 Jake and the lorry drivers
Individual answers